PRAISE FOR *HEALING FROM GREAT LOSS*

"An extremely helpful and enlightening book for enriching one's healing odyssey through grief...Ann compassionately reveals to us that there are many gifts emerging from a great loss just waiting to be discovered, and satisfying the soul's longing for a life to be lived more fully."

—Elizabeth Watson, CHt, PLRt, LBLt, CRMT, NCC, former editor of the Michael Newton Institute's journal *Stories of the Afterlife*

"It is not often that we come across a book as profound as Ann Clark's *Healing from Great Loss*...It is perfect for anyone trying to understand and appreciate the valuable opportunities for growth that life continually offers us and would be invaluable to counsellors and healers."

—Wendy and Victor Zammit, co-authors of *The Friday Afterlife Report*

"Dr. Ann Clark is one of the most brilliant minds I know when it comes to understanding the soul's journey...This book will heal where you thought healing was never possible."

—Tish Murray, The Cheeky Medium

"By sharing her own experience with great loss and her subsequent journey into healing, Ann Clark directs her readers to cultivate growth out of the wounds of loss by opening up to new ways of thinking and living. This book is an invitation to use great loss as a springboard into new dimensions."

—Reverend Dr. Sheri Perl, founder of the Prayer Registry and author of *Lost and Found: A Mother Connects-Up with Her Son in Spirit*

"Ann Clark brings clarity, spiritual breadth, and practicality to navigating the difficult landscape of great loss...If you are looking to find your footing after a great loss, this book offers a perspective that helps to heal the heart, strengthen the mind, and open the way."

—Savarna Wiley, MA, CCHT, hospice chaplain and Michael Newton Institute–certified Life between Lives hypnotherapist/trainer

"*Healing from Great Loss* will take you on a journey filled with compassion, wisdom, insight, guidance, and personal examples and stories…Ann's wisdom, along with her own personal story, gives you the opportunity to hold a new perspective, make peace with your loss, and have hope for the future, no matter where you are on your journey. This is a book that can set you free."

—Betsey Grady, psychic medium

"Dr. Clark has brilliantly crafted this guidebook that is personal and instructive simultaneously. This is a gift to the grieving, not just for great loss, but for all grief and loss which follows change within our lives."

—Maggie W. Banger, LPC-S, NCC, certified grief recovery specialist through the Grief Recovery Institute

"The mix of earthly and otherworldly wisdom in this book can help you survive and even thrive during life's toughest challenges. I suggest reading this book twice, then sharing it with others."

—Mark Pitstick, author of *Greater Reality Living*

HEALING FROM
GREAT
LOSS

© kpstudios.com

Dr. Ann J. Clark spent most of her career as an academic researcher, most recently at the University of Alabama at Birmingham, where she directed the Center for Nursing Research. A sought-after speaker on the afterlife, she is a Michael Newton Institute–certified Life between Lives facilitator and a Reiki Master. She is the owner of and practices at Wisdom for Wellness in Hoover, Alabama. Her popular Great Loss workshops are offered online. She holds a BS in nursing from Macalester College and an MN from Emory University and is a registered nurse. Her PhD is from the University of Chicago. She is the author of numerous professional publications. Previous books that she has coauthored are *Llewellyn's Little Book of Life Between Lives* and *Wisdom of Souls,* winner of a 2020 Coalition of Visionary Resources Gold Book Award. She is the recipient of numerous awards, among them the prestigious Peggy Newton Award from the Michael Newton Institute. You can reach her at hypnoannclark@gmail.com or visit her website at www.birminghamhypnosis.com.

HEALING FROM

GREAT
LOSS

FACING PAIN AND GRIEF TO RECOVER YOUR AUTHENTIC SELF

ANN J. CLARK PhD, RN

FOREWORD BY PETER SMITH
FORMER PRESIDENT OF MICHAEL NEWTON INSTITUTE

LLEWELLYN PUBLICATIONS
WOODBURY, MINNESOTA

FIRST EDITION
First Printing, 2021

Cover design by Shannon McKuhen
Photo on page viii © Ann J. Clark

Llewellyn Publications is a registered trademark of Llewellyn Worldwide Ltd.

Library of Congress Cataloging-in-Publication Data
Names: Clark, Ann J., author.
Title: Healing from great loss : facing pain and grief to recover your
    authentic self / by Ann J Clark, PhD, RN.
Description: First edition. | Woodbury, Minnesota : Llewellyn Worldwide,
    2021. | Includes bibliographical references. | Summary: "This book
    chronicles the author's journey back to herself and provides a road map
    for understanding and healing from a great loss, in which we have lost
    our sense of identity and/or life direction. It is envisioned as the
    soul's invitation to return to the purpose we have set for this life,
    after we have lost our way"— Provided by publisher.
Identifiers: LCCN 2021036009 (print) | LCCN 2021036010 (ebook) | ISBN
    9780738766898 (paperback) | ISBN 9780738767086 (ebook)
Subjects: LCSH: Loss (Psychology) | Grief. | Motivation (Psychology)
Classification: LCC BF575.D35 C53 2021 (print) | LCC BF575.D35 (ebook) |
    DDC 155.9/3—dc23
LC record available at https://lccn.loc.gov/2021036009
LC ebook record available at https://lccn.loc.gov/2021036010

Llewellyn Publications
A Division of Llewellyn Worldwide Ltd.
2143 Wooddale Drive
Woodbury, MN 55125-2989
www.llewellyn.com

Printed in the United States of America

OTHER BOOKS BY ANN J. CLARK, PHD, RN

Wisdom of Souls:
Case Studies of Life Between Lives
from the Michael Newton Institute
(coauthored with Karen Joy, Joanne Selinske,
and Marilyn Hargreaves, Llewellyn, 2019)

Llewellyn's Little Book of Life Between Lives
(coauthored with the Michael Newton Institute,
Llewellyn, 2018)

DEDICATION

This book is a tribute to the soul who was my precious daughter Stefani. She returned home to the spirit realm on November 13, 2016. As I write this, so many wonderful memories are flooding my mind. I remember that first moment our eyes met in the delivery room right after her birth. A fierce, tender motherly love struck me like a thunderbolt. I remember all the poignant moments throughout her childhood and the pride I felt as I watched her grow into a beautiful young woman, and how honored I was to be her mother. A strong friendship blossomed between us as she reached adulthood. When she offered me her sage advice, she would look at me lovingly and say, "I have to tell you about yourself, because no one else will!" After her departure, I wondered, Who is going to tell me about myself now? That is, until one day, when I was sitting out in the sun feeling sorry for myself, and a distinct voice broke into my musings: *I am going to have to tell you about yourself.*

Stefani

CONTENTS

EXERCISES

ACKNOWLEDGMENTS

Writing this book has been very healing for me and I am grateful to those who assisted me with this project. I want to thank Angela Wix, the staff from Llewellyn, and the patients and workshop participants who allowed me to use their stories. I am grateful to Dr. Patricia Fares-O'Malley and Maureen Perkins, who joined me in offering the first Great Loss workshop and for their thoughtful reviews. I would also like to thank Dr. Juanzetta Flowers and Dr. Victoria Moore for their helpful comments.

DISCLAIMER

The information in this book is designed to provide helpful information about healing from significant loss. It is not intended to be, nor should it be used as, a substitute for the advice and care of professional health-care providers or licensed professional counselors. The reader is advised to consult these professionals for matters related to their physical or mental health, particularly those signs and symptoms that may require diagnosis and treatment.

FOREWORD

I remember well the moment I met Dr. Ann Clark. We were preparing the training room at the San Damiano Retreat Center outside of San Francisco, ready to undertake an incredible week of training for the Michael Newton Institute. Ann came through with her bag, looking for her room down the corridor. I sense now that in that moment our souls smiled at each other, knowing what was to come in our work together.

The author of this book is a remarkable person for many reasons, though for me her accomplishments at the Michael Newton Institute have been profound. She created our research department under the robust guidelines that must always be present to be successful. She oversaw the creation of two books for our organization, the first at the direct invitation of Dr. Michael Newton himself, as he handed the baton to Ann to take his life's work to the world through the written word.

The second book was a compilation of many cases into a practical volume of inspiring Life between Lives stories containing wisdom for living, which was Ann's idea from start to finish. Michael's passion had become Ann's, and it came as no surprise to anyone that she was awarded the

Peggy Newton Award for outstanding service to the Michael Newton Institute. This is an award that has been given only a handful of times over the years and is the highest honor our organization can bestow.

Throughout all this, Ann suffered the greatest tragedy a parent can ever know when she lost her daughter. I witnessed just a small amount of the pain she endured and eventually transcended. It was a journey that was literally multidimensional in all its complexity.

When Ann mentioned that she was to write this book, there was something in the background that stirred for me ever so gently, just outside my line of sight. It was like there was a knowing that once again Ann was creating something of magnitude to serve humanity in ways that she may not even realize. There it was, a powerful and extraordinary way to observe, embrace, and honor the experience of human grief from a transcended perspective.

Here was the perfect person to offer this sacred gift to anyone who has dealt with great loss: a powerful intellect, honed through the world of academia, combined with the passion of a spiritual explorer of the afterlife, grounded in the deep and heartfelt experience of living with great loss.

This book is far more than that story, however. Ann brings her experience as a nurse to this endeavor. As anyone who has ever met a life-long nurse will tell you, it is not a profession, but a calling. It is a desire to serve humanity through the gentle presence that nursing brings, offering the compassion and service that it takes to help someone heal.

This book carries all of the above, though it was born of the desire to serve others that is part of the character of this author. I feel that it comes from the human being who pulled these words together, as much as the intention of the immortal presence that shares the form. I know in my heart that this book is a gift to the world and will help countless numbers of people deal with the challenges they face as they move through their own great loss.

For me, that day in the training room near San Francisco was one of those moments when you cross paths with an exceptional person. Even though I did not yet know Ann well in human form, my meeting with her echoed something deeper in me that this was someone of significance who had been brought to our institute to do something that no one else could. As I have the great honor to write these words, I sense our souls smiling at each other once again.

You have in your possession a remarkable book written by a special person. May it serve you well, from the pure intention in which it was written.

—Peter Smith
President of the Michael Newton Institute, 2009–2019

INTRODUCTION

If you have experienced a serious loss—such as the loss of a loved one, a divorce, the loss of health or physical function, job loss, or financial disaster—and are having a hard time getting over it, then this book is for you. I experienced a devastating loss with the unexpected death of my adult daughter, my only child, several years ago.

While I had experienced other losses in my life, nothing impacted me the way losing my daughter did. A divorce years earlier, the loss of my mother, and most recently, the loss of my youngest brother were all painful losses, but this one was different. It felt as if the very foundation of my life had crumbled and I did not know how to pick up the pieces and go on.

I have always found the advice in books helpful at difficult times in my life, and I searched desperately for ones that would help me then. I did find several that were helpful in the early stages of my grief, but later I needed something more. I wanted to find a book that acknowledged what I believe to be our true reality as Souls who have incarnated on earth to grow spiritually, one that would help me make sense of the tragedy that had blindsided me. I also wanted to learn why this loss hurt so much worse that those that proceeded it and how to relieve the pain that I was experiencing.

That book was nowhere to be found. I vowed that if I were able to successfully move beyond this disaster, I would share the path to healing that I had discovered. I experienced several major breakthroughs in my understanding of loss from the Soul's perspective as I struggled to regain my footing in the world. I also gained a new perspective on the physical, emotional, and mental toll that a great loss exerts on our being.

I call this type of loss *great loss* because it turns our world upside down and steals our sense of security and our sense of place in the world. I came to realize that this type of loss, while common, is not well understood. A different perspective was needed for me to grasp the meaning that losses of this type have on our lives and to realize the spiritual gift that is embedded in the experience. Considering loss from the Soul's perspective was the key.

I learned that great loss comes into our lives when we are stuck in patterns that are limiting our spiritual growth. The loss frees us from these limiting patterns and enables us to return to pursuing the plans we made for our current life on earth. The gift in this experience is the opportunity to become our authentic self and achieve renewed fulfillment and joy in our lives. However, first we must heal, and this book will show you how.

There are thousands of books available on loss, many of which are helpful for those experiencing serious loss and for those of us experiencing great loss in its early stages. However, to work our way through great loss and its aftermath, we need some additional assistance. This book picks up where the other books on grief have left off to fill that gap.

While the first stages of grief from great loss are like those experienced in all significant losses, there is more for us to heal before we regain our equilibrium. While all individuals who have experienced loss must learn to live without the person or thing they have lost, our adjustment is more complicated. We have lost a piece of our core identity and security. We must rebuild our lives from the foundation, because they have been upended.

This book is unique among those about grieving and loss. What makes this one different is that it

- addresses the kind of loss that shatters our world, robbing us of our sense of safety, stability, and self-assurance;
- describes significant loss from the perspective of the Soul;
- speaks to loss that occurs when we are not in touch with our inner guidance and are stuck in patterns that limit our spiritual growth; and
- offers specific strategies to heal from the loss, enabling us to recover our authentic self and find renewed fulfillment and joy in our lives.

Great loss feels so devastating because it deprives us of our source of certainty and confidence in an uncertain world. It takes from us someone or something that we cannot bear to lose. It robs us of what we view as making our life worth living. Great loss causes us to question what is meaningful in our lives. At the same time, great loss is a spiritual gift, one that can help us build soul character and lead more fulfilling lives.

Perhaps we have lost a person central to our well-being. Or perhaps we have lost our career, our faith, or our health, or have experienced an unfulfilled expectation central to our lives. It could be that we are focusing too strongly on someone or something outside of ourselves. Or it could be that we are so distracted living a busy life that we lose track of who we are and where we are going. Or perhaps we have fallen into an undemanding lifestyle in which we have traded comfort and security for true fulfillment. Whatever the case, great loss stops us in our tracks.

OUR TRUE IDENTITY AS SOULS

As Souls, our true home is in the spirit world. We choose to incarnate on earth to build Soul character and to advance spiritually. We can view coming here as going away to school. We plan our life circumstances and what we want to learn as if we were planning a course of study. We have done this many times before through the self-improvement process of reincarnation. What we do not learn in one life, we carry over to the next.

We join with a human body of our choice each time we incarnate, and the *conscious self*, or *ego*, allows us to interact and participate in life on earth. We incarnate with a portion of our Soul energy that resides within us as our *Higher Self*. Our Higher Self provides us with subtle inner guidance while we are living on earth. This is important, as we forget who we are and why we came here once we have incarnated. This inner guidance serves to keep us on track as we pursue our life purpose.

GREAT LOSS IN OUR LIVES

Great loss occurs at a time when we are chugging along with a false sense of well-being because we are not in touch with this inner guidance and living as our authentic self. Thus, we are disconnected from the internal compass that helps us steer our ship during our earth journey—our Higher Self—and we are traveling blindly. When the loss occurs, it knocks us completely out of our comfort zone and leaves us panicked, confused, and disheartened.

Not all losses that we experience in our lives will affect us in this way. While all losses are painful and require some adjustment, not all of them shake our very foundation. Our security can be disturbed by a great loss because we lose someone or something outside of ourselves that we regard as essential to our welfare. In contrast, when we are in sync with our Higher (or true) Self and living as our authentic self, nothing can shake our foundation.

Great loss, as depicted in this book, comes when patterns in our life are limiting our Soul growth or when we are living life on the surface rather than venturing deep inside to live life as our true self. It comes at a time when we are disconnected from our inner guidance and are focused on someone or something outside of ourselves, or just not focused at all.

The loss is not an unfortunate twist of fate or a punishment for ignoring our inner guidance, however. Rather, the loss is an invitation from our Soul self to remember what we came to earth to accomplish this time. It is an invitation to integrate our conscious self, or ego, with our Higher Self and begin living life on earth as our authentic, or true, self.

We receive this invitation because when we planned our current life, we set the intention for this to be one in which we make significant spiritual progress. We asked to be alerted should we get off track or become stalled in reaching our goals. Accepting the invitation to integrate our conscious self with our Higher Self will allow us to get back to our own life path. This will provide guidance to us in fulfilling our life purpose and will also bring greater joy and happiness into our lives.

Lest you conclude that a lack of connection with your inner guidance at the time of your loss caused it, let me hasten to correct that misconception. There are many people who sail through life without access to their inner guidance and never experience a significant loss. We have free will and can choose to disregard the promptings of our Higher Self.

Failure to acknowledge the subtle voice of our Higher Self does not cause loss; it just results in us going through life without the guidance that is available to us. When we fail to tune in to our inner guidance, we reduce the chances that we will stay on track and accomplish the goals that we set for this lifetime. Our disconnection from this inner guidance does not cause our loss, but when great loss occurs, we are off course or stalled in pursuing spiritual growth.

Our loss is a spiritual gift. It is a wake-up call from our Higher Self, reminding us to make the most of the days that we have left on earth.

This misfortune is an event that can free us from limiting patterns in our life and give us a second chance to achieve the purpose that we chose for our current incarnation.

Thus, if we choose to accept this gift, our lives can be better than ever, and we will grow immeasurably as Souls. There is much healing we will do along the way. I will show you how in the pages that follow.

Using my own story and those of friends, colleagues, and patients from my practice in spiritual hypnotherapy, I will help you gain an understanding of the spiritual meaning of great loss in your life. I will provide guidance to help you grasp the opportunity for significant spiritual growth and greater happiness that this type of loss offers.

To protect the privacy of those who have shared their stories with me, I have created composite accounts of fictional characters, sticking as closely as possible to the real experiences. I have also included some cases of relevant Life between Lives sessions conducted by me as a Michael Newton Institute Life between Lives facilitator, with permission of the patients.

I forewarn you about the potential long-term effects of this type of loss so that you can be prepared to avoid or minimize them. Great loss breaks us open and reveals all the previous losses in our lives that we have not resolved. While this can be painful, it creates just the right circumstances to allow us to heal. Most importantly, I assure you that contained within your loss is the opportunity to make your life even better than it was before.

I map out the route that helped me gain an understanding of my loss and move forward in my life with renewed energy. Also included are specific suggestions that you can follow to heal from your great loss. Those of us who have experienced a great loss have lived through great pain, but have also had the good fortune to have loved deeply and/or experienced great passion.

We will always remember the love and/or passion we experienced, but the pain of our loss will greatly lessen over time. The good news is that not only is it possible to grow beyond our loss, but the life that follows can be even more fulfilling than it was before. While the loss we have experienced has been very traumatic, we can heal from it by facing our pain and grief. The message of this book is that we can successfully integrate this loss into our lives and achieve significant spiritual growth and happiness.

Through accepting this Soul invitation, we can recover our authentic Self, making our lives richer and more meaningful. I want you to know that you are not alone in this journey. We have much to look forward to in the future when we choose to heal and grow from our loss.

One word of caution: If your loss has been very recent and you are still reeling from the shock and strong emotions that follow any significant loss, put this book aside for a while. This is not a book for those in the early stages of adjusting to a loss. Rather, it is what is needed when we have passed through the shock and acute pain of the loss and are left feeling anxious, empty, and deeply disappointed with the turn that our life has taken. It is what we need when we realize that we have survived and are questioning, "What do I do now?" When you are ready, I am here to guide you on your road to a new life.

AFTER THE LOSS

While it is easier to make no active changes after we have survived the early stages of mourning and just try to get by, unless we seek to heal and learn from the experience, we will suffer needlessly. We will also be passing up a unique opportunity to find greater fulfillment in our lives and achieve significant spiritual progress. Modifying our circumstances alone, in the absence of healing measures, is not sufficient to ease our aching heart. Likewise, jumping into something else right away might make the pain go away temporarily, but it will not help us grow from our loss into a better life.

This is a bewildering time, and no one knows better what we need to move forward and learn to live in our new reality than we do ourselves. The key is to connect with our inner guidance and the spiritual assistance available to us. This will lead us to healing and a renewed zest for living. It can also save us from the potential pitfalls that lie ahead.

For example, we could slip into bitterness and disillusionment—not a very pleasant place to be. We could also go on just living on the surface, by allowing the ever-changing conditions in our everyday life to shape us. Or we could get stuck in patterns that limit our spiritual growth again.

It all sounds scary, but the solution is simple: by connecting with our inner guidance, we will have a light to guide us to a more fulfilling life, one in which we can make significant spiritual advancement and find joy.

WHAT THIS BOOK COVERS

In chapter 1, I tell you the story of my great loss. The death of my precious daughter was unexpected and could not have come at a worse time. I was hospitalized for knee surgery when it happened and had never been both so physically and emotionally miserable in my life. My belief in our identity as Souls and my knowledge of the afterlife were central to my understanding of and healing from this loss. I share with you my road to healing and what really helped me find peace and renewed energy for living.

In chapter 2, life on earth is described from the Soul's perspective. What we have learned from the work of Dr. Michael Newton, whose extensive research informs us about our lives as Souls both on earth and in our true home in the spirit world, is discussed. Dr. Newton is the developer of the Life between Lives technique and the author of several books, including *Journey of Souls* and *Destiny of Souls*. New information that has emerged from the over 65,000 Life between Lives sessions that have been performed by Michael Newton Institute members worldwide is also included. Why we choose to come to earth and how we carefully plan each lifetime is discussed. The system of spiritual guidance that is available to us while living on earth is also explained.

In chapter 3, great loss is defined and differentiated from other losses that we may have experienced in our lives. Great loss takes from us what has been the center of our lives and what gives us a sense of security, purpose, and/or belongingness. The loss comes at a time when we either have become stuck in patterns that keep us from moving forward on our Soul's journey or are too complacent or distracted with the busyness of our lives to be aware of our inner guidance. This sets the stage for chapter 4, which defines loss from the Soul's perspective.

There is no loss in the spirit world, a place of peace, love, and harmony. Loss is an experience that the Soul seeks during an earth incarnation for the spiritual growth that it can produce. There are multiple reasons why we might plan a significant loss, such as experiencing the pain of loss so that we can help others with grieving in the future or seeking karmic balance in our life experiences. We may have made a contract with another Soul to participate in a life that includes a painful separation or betrayal that will provide learning for both of us.

A great loss is a rude awakening that provides us with an opportunity to evaluate how we are using our current lifetime. The loss is also a spiritual gift that gives us a unique chance to change direction and get back to our own life plans. Chapter 4 describes great loss as an event that we include in our life planning to rescue us should we lose track of our life purpose in a life in which we intend to gain significant spiritual growth. In my case, and maybe yours too, the primary Soul lesson for this lifetime was contained within the pattern in which I had become stuck. I will explain that fully in chapter 11.

There comes a time, after our loss and the emotional roller coaster that we have been on, when something begins stirring within us that urges us to get back to a more normal existence. This is a time when we have a choice to make, although it is largely unconscious. This is a defining moment, a point at which we make a decision that will dramatically affect the rest of our lives.

This is the point at which we can choose to accept the invitation from our Soul-self to align with who we truly are and learn the lessons we came to master during this lifetime. Defining moments are discussed in chapter 5. We may not know when our defining moments are coming, but we can prepare for them. Information is provided on how to prepare for defining moments. Cases are presented that show us that we generally have more than one opportunity to revisit this choice, if we have not made it in our own best interest.

An important part of healing from great loss is addressing the effects of our loss on our physical self. Loss can precipitate long-term difficulties in sleeping, eating, and feeling at ease in our lives. Fatigue can be prolonged. The incidence of serious illness or injury is increased in the two to six years following a loss. Chapter 6 discusses the long-term physical effects of loss and offers strategies for coping with them.

Chapter 7 discusses the long-term psychological effects of great loss. A loss of confidence, energy, and/or motivation and a temporary difficulty in relating to others are often present. The world no longer seems as safe or manageable as it once did. Anxiety is often an issue. The effort to cling to our old life following a loss is understandable, but that option is no longer there.

Attempts to rearrange things to recreate life as it was before the loss as closely as possible are generally unsatisfying. There is a danger that we may slip into a distraction such as food, alcohol, or work, or we may overdo computer time, TV watching, reading, exercising, or socializing. Sooner or later, we come to the realization that the distraction is not working and that a new direction is needed. Managing the psychological aftereffects of great loss is discussed in chapter 7.

The spiritual gift of great loss is discussed in chapter 8. Our loss knocks us out of our comfort zone and gives us a chance to reflect on where our life is going. This provides us with an opportunity to change direction and reflect on what we hope to accomplish in our lives. It also gives us the time and the opportunity to connect with our Higher Self and the spiritual guidance that is available to us.

Chapter 9 discusses how we can heal the wounds that are both created and revealed by our loss. To move successfully into the future, we must heal the wounds that have been exposed by our loss. While great loss leads us to a doorway to a happier, more fulfilling life, it also opens us up to old wounds that have not been healed. This can result in some deep emotional suffering if we do not address them. This pain does not go away with the passage of time. Thus, we must face our pain and grief. This is a time to engage in maximum self-care as we heal.

We need to go back and heal the old wounds that are revealed by our current loss. Action is necessary to resolve this sorrow and regain a sense of well-being. We may need to forgive others, offer apologies as needed, and perhaps forgive ourselves. If we have lost a loved one, part of our healing may involve noticing the signs that they are still with us. We may also wish to reestablish communication with our departed loved one. Instructions for doing so are presented in chapter 9.

Chapter 10 discusses how we can learn life-changing lessons from our loss. Assessing our lives before our loss and looking for meaning in our lives can assist us in finding our life lessons. Included are Life between Lives cases that illustrate the profound learning that can follow a great loss. Successfully healing from a great loss by aligning our conscious self with our Higher Self leads to a life that is more joyful, authentic, and fulfilling. We become fully alive and open to all that life on earth has to offer on our Soul journey.

In chapter 11, I discuss the powerful lesson I learned through the painful experience of great loss. I have included the Life between Lives session that enabled me to put this learning together and integrate it into my life. I present this as an example. Your lessons will be different. I offer you suggestions to follow in finding and learning yours.

Lastly, I want to leave you with some inspiration. Not only is it possible for you to survive your great loss, but you can make your life better than ever. In chapter 12, I share the case of one of my patients who successfully healed after a difficult divorce. While great loss is very painful, it frees us from patterns that were limiting our spiritual growth. After such a significant loss, we can set off in a new direction and go after our forgotten hopes and dreams. Connecting with our inner guidance lights our path and shows us the way.

HOW TO USE THIS BOOK

This book will be most helpful if you read it in the order in which it is presented. At the end of some chapters you will find a summary of suggestions for healing. You will also find suggested exercises at the end of each chapter. Please have a notebook available to record your experiences with these exercises and to journal your thoughts and feelings as you move along through the book. Additional resources are available at www.healingfromgreatloss.com.

I will be with you in spirit each step of the way. With great compassion, I wish you well on your healing journey.

CHAPTER ONE
MY GREAT LOSS

November 13, 2016, was the worst day of my life! It was my third postoperative day following knee surgery, the day any nurse will tell you is one of the most difficult. But that paled in comparison to what happened next. That was the day I experienced my great loss. My adult daughter, my only child, died unexpectedly that day, and it felt like a large part of me died along with her.

THE STORY OF MY GREAT LOSS

Eight years prior to her death, my daughter was brutally raped and robbed. She developed post-traumatic stress syndrome with agoraphobia, severe anxiety, and depression in the aftermath of this event. Agoraphobia is an anxiety disorder in which individuals avoid situations and places where they might feel trapped. This condition became so difficult for my daughter that she became afraid to leave the house. This condition can last for several years or even be lifelong.

Feeling helpless, I brought my daughter home to live with me again. She was under the care of a psychiatrist and heavily medicated to control her symptoms. My heart went out to her, as she seemed so vulnerable and broken. Just about my every waking moment became dedicated to helping her recover.

It is not that I quit my practice in spiritual hypnotherapy and suspended all my other activities. No, I continued just as before, or so it must have looked from the outside. However, her well-being became the focus of my world. That was the basis upon which I planned my days. When things were not going well for her, nothing was right for me either. My main responsibility became helping her recover. I continued with my own endeavors, but my heart was not in them.

Things would start to get better and then they would get worse. She broke her leg and had asthma attacks, dental problems, and all sorts of minor health issues. She became so fearful that she was afraid to answer the door. We spent several birthdays and holidays in a hospital emergency room. I became more and more desperate to find a way to help her. I felt that as her mother, it was my responsibility to do so, and that with my professional background, I should be able to manage it. My anxiety rose, as there seemed to be no long-term improvement.

Meanwhile, I was trying to keep up with everything else. This put stress on my relationship with my long-term romantic partner, and I was exhausted and discouraged a good bit of the time. My daughter was depressed nearly all the time, and I tried so hard to raise her spirits.

Things were at their lowest point when she met a boyfriend on the internet. They established a relationship through online chats and became quite close. For the first time since her brutal attack, she was willing to go out with someone, and they started seeing each other. The relationship was chaotic and unstable. She experienced extraordinary highs and lows for the short time that it lasted. She started taking extra anxiety medication during her low periods, and I became alarmed.

She finally could take no more and ended the relationship. Afterward she was even more depressed and seemed to retreat into herself. I feared that she was becoming addicted to her prescription medications. I just kept trying even harder.

It was a difficult summer, but she seemed to finally make some significant progress. She started thinking about her future, and my hopes soared. We worked together to reduce her dependence on her anxiety medications, and she made solid progress in doing so. She seemed so much better that I felt comfortable having the knee surgery I had been putting off. She started making plans for the future and even started looking for a job.

We talked about my upcoming surgery, and she shared her plans for cooking and taking care of me when I returned home. I was heartened by her enthusiasm and looked forward to spending this special time with her after my hospitalization, when our caretaking roles would be reversed. As I prepared for my surgery, I remember thinking that a brighter future was on the way.

She spent two nights with me in the hospital after my surgery and seemed more relaxed than I had seen her in a long time. She joked about making sure I did all the exercises. I was able to walk with her to the elevator as she left that morning, and the last thing we said to each other was "I love you."

I was not able to reach her later that day, but I assumed that she was sleeping. I became a little worried when she still did not respond the following morning. I was about to call my partner and ask him to stop and check on her on his way in to visit me when I experienced a frightening event.

I had been resting after breakfast before my scheduled physical therapy session when I started feeling weak, dizzy, and slightly nauseated. The situation worsened and I was about to call for assistance when I realized that I was too weak to move. Even breathing became an effort, and I had a sudden awareness that I was dying. Interestingly, I felt no apprehension, but rather just a peaceful sense of inevitability.

I am not sure how long this went on, because there was a sense of timelessness, but it probably was no more than fifteen to twenty minutes. Then suddenly all the symptoms went away as quickly as they had come on, and I felt normal again. The nurse examined me and checked my vital signs, and all were normal. We were puzzled by this event.

As soon as my partner arrived, I sent him to check on my daughter. He did not return for what seemed like a long time, and again I became worried. I was shocked when he returned with the news that he had found her lying on her bed, unresponsive. He immediately called for assistance, and she was pronounced dead at the scene. I do not really remember much about the next few hours, as I went into shock.

At first, we had no idea what had happened to my daughter. Since her inhaler had been found next to her, we were told tentatively that the cause of death might be related to her asthma, but an autopsy was to be performed. The coroner estimated the time of death to be between 9:00 and 11:00 that morning. I knew right away exactly when it had happened, as I realized instinctively that it had been the cause of my unsettling episode that morning. I had experienced a type of shared death experience, although I did not realize what it was as it was happening.

Shared death experiences have traditionally been described as profound spiritual experiences of onlookers by the side of the dying person. They might report seeing the dying person's spirit leaving the body and they may accompany the dying person partway toward the light.[1] William Peters, founder and executive director of Shared Crossing Project, is studying a wide range of experiences that individuals may have before, during, and after the death of another.[2] The physical experience that I had—in a different location and without the knowledge that a death was occurring—is reported less often and is a very interesting phenomenon.

---

1. Raymond Moody Jr., with Paul Perry, *Glimpses of Eternity* (New York: Guideposts, 2010).

2. William Peters, "What Are Shared Crossings?," Shared Crossing Project, accessed August 7, 2021, https://www.sharedcrossing.com/shared-crossings.html.

THE SPECIAL BOND
BETWEEN PARENT AND CHILD

I remember a patient of mine who lost her youngest son.

My patient's son had been through a difficult divorce several years before his unexpected death, but had been doing well. He had completed his degree in physical therapy and had a job at a rehabilitation center that he loved and a group of close friends. When he didn't show up for work on Monday, his coworkers went to check on him and found that he had died sometime over the weekend. There was no apparent cause of death, and authorities were uncertain about when it had happened. No one had seen him or heard from him since Friday evening, when he had been out with his friends.

My patient claimed that she knew exactly when her son had died. She had suddenly become violently ill during her Sunday morning church service, and then her symptoms just disappeared as suddenly as they had come on. As a single parent, she was close to her children and thought perhaps her daughter, who was expecting her first child at any time, must have gone into labor. When she learned of her son's death, however, she knew right away that her sudden illness had come on at the time of his death.

After meeting that patient, I asked other parents who had experienced an unexpected death of one of their children whether they'd had any unusual experiences at the time of their child's death. I have not encountered any other cases. There is little in the literature about this occurrence, but I think it warrants further study.

Over the years, scientists and child development specialists have discovered that the bond between parent and child is one of the strongest connections in nature. There have been documented cases of telecommunication between mothers and children and reports that mothers just have a "knowing" when their child is in trouble.

Another interesting finding is that scientists have discovered children's cells living in their mother's brain. The term *microchimerism* describes the persistent presence of a few genetically distinct cells in an organism. This most commonly results from the exchange of cells across the placenta. The connection between mother and child may be even deeper than thought.

AFTER MY GREAT LOSS

The period following the news of my daughter's death was one of the most difficult times in my entire life. Perhaps because I was in a weakened state, having just gone through a surgical procedure, I experienced a severe reaction and only later realized that I had gone into shock. I felt numb, as if I were seeing and hearing what was going on around me from a distance. I did come out of this initial state in only a few hours, feeling as if someone had splashed a bucket of ice water on me to wake me up.

The staff at the rehabilitation center were very sympathetic. They moved the other bed out of my room and brought in extra chairs for my friends and family who came to offer me support. I was unable to sleep or eat much during the next few days that I spent there. The reaction to this loss was much more severe than what I had experienced with previous losses.

The entire first two years after my daughter's death were difficult, and I cried at least once every day during that period. There were some things I did during that time, however, that were helpful. We are fortunate to have an excellent community grief center in the area in which I live, and I took advantage of their free services. Initially I started seeing a grief counselor at the center, one who was very well trained and helpful. I really looked forward to the sessions. Even though at the beginning I cried for most of the time we were together, I always felt better when I left.

The second thing I did at the community grief center was join a group of parents who had lost adult children. I was fortunate that the group leader not only encouraged us to share our feelings but gave us helpful information as well. It was tremendously comforting to hear from the other parents and know that I was not alone in struggling to deal with the crippling grief that consumed me.

It was while I was attending the group that the news came that my daughter had died of a drug overdose. While I had feared earlier that she might have been addicted to her prescription medications, I was unaware that she was ever taking more than that. Other parents in the group were going through the same experience, and being able to talk about it freely and hear my feelings reflected in their comments was remarkably comforting.

As time went on, I became more aware of the strong feelings that were underneath my tears. Following my divorce, my daughter and I had become our own small family of two. As she grew to adulthood, we each moved on with our lives, but we remained close. Despite each of us developing romantic relationships and close friendships, we still considered this small family our anchor.

I was appalled and devastated upon learning of her sudden death. I expected that we would remain close as I aged, and that no matter how far away she lived or whatever other close relationships we formed, our special love and companionship would always be central to our lives. It was not supposed to be this way! I was not sure I would ever get over such a catastrophic loss.

The fact that I was a certified Life between Lives facilitator through the Michael Newton Institute and knew a lot about death and dying did little to mitigate my pain in those early days. I was inconsolable and fell into a deep depression. However, later that knowledge was the very thing that helped me climb out of a deep well of despair.

During those first two years, I recognized the commonly reported stages of grieving that I was moving in and out of, and eventually the acute pain did lessen. Still, I experienced no real relief. My zest for living was gone, and although I was going through the motions, my world was gray and lifeless.

While I was having no difficulty in coping with everyday life, I felt dead inside. It became obvious to me that nothing was going to change unless I did something about it. However, my energy was low at this point, and part of me just did not care enough to take any action. It felt like I was moving through mud, and my days just dragged on.

This went on for some time before I started feeling restless. It was then that I decided I had to choose to heal and take some action to make it happen. Over the next year, I did just that.

INSIGHTS I GAINED FROM GREAT LOSS

Along the way, I gained many insights about loss and how it impacts the Soul's journey. I learned that there is a common thread that delineates all great losses, whether it be the death of a loved one, a divorce, career disruption, financial ruin, or a health crisis.

I came to understand that the Soul who had been my daughter had decided that it was time to go home. She was still with me, just in a different way. The love that we shared was still there. I learned that she had been with me and had been trying to comfort me during those difficult early days after her death. Along the way on my healing journey, I learned to reestablish communication with her.

My healing journey has not been a smooth one and has taken longer and been much more difficult than I anticipated. The pain has been intense at times, but the spiritual growth and understanding that I have gained from experiencing this loss has been appreciable. The pain of great loss does last longer than it does for other losses, and we must work harder to heal. However, the potential rewards for putting in the time and effort to do so are considerable.

Great loss frees us from patterns that were limiting our spiritual growth and thus keeping us from being fully engaged in pursuing our own hopes and dreams. We now can live our best lives yet and make the most of the time we have left here on earth. I share my healing journey and what I learned along the way with you in the pages that follow. You will find specific strategies to employ on your own healing journey. I wish you well!

EXERCISE

TELL THE STORY OF YOUR GREAT LOSS

Record the story of your great loss in a notebook. Write about your reactions and feelings as well as the events. Include as much detail as you would like. Write about the following:

- Any events leading up to your loss
- How you learned of your loss
- What happened
- How the events surrounding your loss unfolded
- What occurred in the early period after your loss
- The longer-term reactions you are having to your loss

CHAPTER TWO

THE SOUL'S VIEW
OF LIFE ON EARTH

One commonly held belief in Western society is that we are human beings who have a Soul and we have only one life to live. Most religions teach that there is an afterlife, but there is still a lot of uncertainty about what happens after we die. Most Western physicians and many scientists still believe that consciousness is generated by the brain and that all awareness ends at the time of death, despite mounting evidence to the contrary. People in other parts of the world have a broader view and are more accepting of the idea of life after death.

MY INTRODUCTION TO THE AFTERLIFE

You have probably heard reports of near-death experiences, stories of mediums who talk with the departed, and news reports of cutting-edge research on consciousness and the nature of reality. Even so, you may still be wondering, Is there really anything at all after we die?

That is no longer a question for me. Many years ago, when I was first introduced to the idea that we live on after the death of our body, something resonated with that truth deep inside of me. Later, when I was working at a busy metropolitan emergency room on weekends while I finished graduate school, I had an experience that cemented the idea in my mind.

> *A middle-aged woman was brought in by ambulance following a horrific automobile accident. She had sustained multiple injuries, was not breathing, and had no pulse when she arrived. She was rushed into a treatment room, and the team set to work frantically trying to resuscitate her. We were successful, and I stayed with her as we prepared to admit her to the hospital.*
>
> *Despite sedation and pain medication, she seemed anxious to tell me about her experience. She related that she had watched us from up above the whole time we had been working on her. I was surprised at how accurate she seemed to be, but assumed that she had seen it on television or been told about those procedures. She sensed that I was not believing her and became upset. As the medical assistant came to take her up to her room, she called back to me, "I saw that big runner you have all the way down your left stocking."*
>
> *I discounted her claim, as she had been unconscious when she was brought into the emergency room, and since she had regained consciousness, I had been at her side as she lay on the cart, so she could not possibly have seen me from the back. And furthermore, I was wearing new pantyhose. It was not until the end of that busy shift, when one of the other nurses asked me what had happened to the back of my stocking, that I looked back and there it was. I got chills!*

My curiosity spurred me to explore similar experiences I had heard about over the years. Initially I dismissed most of these stories as being the result of side effects of medications or artifacts of the dying brain. I joke now that after about the hundredth episode, I began to think that there might just be something to it. However, I put this data on the back burner. It just did not fit in with my plans to finish my education and become a nurse researcher. But as I completed my PhD and launched my career as an academic researcher, those experiences remained in the back of my mind.

Somewhere around mid-career, I started to feel some disillusionment with the traditional health care system. I developed an interest in mind, body, and spiritual health and became active in alternative therapies and integrative health care. It was not long before existential questions such as "Who are we?" and "What is life all about?" came up for me. That was when I discovered the groundbreaking work of Dr. Michael Newton through his books *Journey of Souls* and *Destiny of Souls*.

The information in Dr. Newton's books helped me realize that what I had been witnessing through the years were near-death experiences. Reading his revelations about who we really are and what we are doing here on earth changed my whole perspective. He reported that through his hypnotherapy sessions with clients, he had discovered that we do not cease to exist after the physical death of our body, but that our consciousness lives on. The truth of what he had discovered resonated deep inside me. It ignited a fire in me to bring this healing knowledge to others.

Later, I took early retirement from the university. In rapid succession, I attained hypnotherapy and past life regression certifications. After some practice, I went on to train and become certified as a Michael Newton Institute Life between Lives facilitator. I have been in private practice since 2007.

I grew up as a Christian with a strong religious background and believe that we are of divine origin. I see the work of Dr. Newton, and the ever-expanding knowledge about the nature of consciousness that is being developed and bringing science and religion closer together, as being consistent with my religious background. My belief in a higher power, God, or a guiding force in the universe remains strong, and I feel guided by this *presence* in the work I do with my patients. I view the material that I share with you in these pages as additional information that has been revealed about who we really are and the nature of our existence, not as conflicting information regarding religious beliefs.

THE WORK OF DR. MICHAEL NEWTON

The vision of how the Soul views life on earth that is covered in this chapter comes from Dr. Newton's work, sessions with my own patients, and reports from the over two hundred certified Life between Lives facilitators across the globe. From this work and that of other pioneers in the field, including Dolores Cannon[3] and Dr. Brian Weiss,[4] we have learned that we are Souls who join with a human body to live lives on earth. We come to earth to have experiences, face challenges, and learn lessons to grow spiritually.

You may be wondering, if this information is true, then why do we not remember who we are and what we are doing here on earth? We have no memory of this because we agree to amnesia when we incarnate so that we can engage fully in life.

We do not cease to exist after our death; only our body dies. Our consciousness as a Soul lives on, and we return to the spirit realm to continue our learning and evolution. Our true home is in the spirit world, the place we came from when we were born and the place we will return to after the death of our current body.

The evolution of the Soul takes more than one lifetime. Through the self-improvement process of reincarnation, we have lived many lives. What we fail to learn or heal in one lifetime is carried over to the next lifetime. We have lived as a different person, in a different body, in each life we have lived. We have lived in many different places and have been many different races and ethnicities. We have been different genders and in many different roles. We have been rich, we have been poor, we have lived extraordinary lives and ordinary lives. The average person I see in my practice has lived between 700 to 1,000 previous lives, some dating back to ancient times.

3. Dolores Cannon, *Between Life and Death* (Huntsville, AR: Ozark Mountain Publishers, 1993).

4. Brian L. Weiss, MD, *Many Lives, Many Masters* (New York: Simon & Schuster, 1988); and *Through Time into Healing* (New York: Simon & Schuster, 1992).

Through his research, Dr. Newton was able to describe the spiritual realm and the activities we engage in as Souls. Many religions tell of an afterlife, usually described as eternal bliss. What Dr. Newton found was that when we die, we return home to the spirit world after the experiences we have had during our life on earth. It is as if we had gone away to school.

While Dr. Newton did find that life in our Soul home is peaceful, loving, and harmonious, it is not a place of eternal rest. Rather, we live full lives there, continuing to evolve as Souls. We live in families or groups with lots of interaction with other Souls. We continue to learn with the assistance of more advanced Souls, engage in meaningful work, pursue creative activities, engage in recreation, and travel throughout the universe.

Some religions describe a hell or state of eternal damnation after death for those who did not live a good life or did not accept the tenets of religion during their lives. Dr. Newton found none of this in his work. Regardless of the lives they have lived, all Souls are able to return home and continue their evolution.

It does not matter if the individual died by suicide, betrayed or cheated others, or committed horrendous acts against humanity. All Souls are welcomed back home when they choose to return. Recovery and rehabilitation are made available as needed. To learn more about life in the spirit world, consult Dr. Newton's books *Journey of Souls* (1994) and *Destiny of Souls* (2000).

Dr. Newton went on to devise a method for individuals to access their Soul self and Soul home while still alive on earth, termed Life between Lives hypnotherapy.[5] Many of the clients he worked with experienced profound healing and were able to develop a new perspective on the challenges in their lives.

---

5. See Michael Newton, *Life Between Lives: Hypnotherapy for Spiritual Regression* (St. Paul, MN: Llewellyn, 2004); and the Michael Newton Institute, Ann J. Clark, Karen Joy, Marilyn Hargreaves, and Joanne Selinske, *Llewellyn's Little Book of Life Between Lives* (Woodbury, MN: Llewellyn, 2018).

Dr. Newton began training others in this method in 2000 and formed an early society to promote the work. In 2005 this became the Michael Newton Institute, and at the time of the writing of this book, there are over two hundred members across the globe trained and certified in the method. Life between Lives sessions are now offered in forty different countries in twenty-four different languages, and it is estimated that 65,000 sessions have been conducted to date.

Dr. Newton made his transition in 2016, but members of the institute continue to carry on this work. A 2015 survey found that Michael Newton Institute members continue to practice according to the method prescribed by Dr. Newton and that results of these sessions are consistent with the findings that he reported.

There is much learning we can do at home in the spirit world, so why do we, as Souls, come to earth to further our advancement? We come to earth to gain new understandings and develop enlightened character traits because of the special opportunities an earth life can provide. When we join with a human body to live a life on earth, we take on the responsibility of supporting ourselves and our families, keeping ourselves safe, and coping with aging, loss, potential illness, injury, or even violence.

We have learned from Dr. Newton's work and our own client sessions that our Soul home is a space of universal harmony, peace, and love. While we may experience these things on earth, we also encounter injustice, suffering, conflict, strong emotions, and pain, providing us with multiple opportunities to grow. The earth experience also provides us with multiple opportunities to use our talents and skills developed thus far to help others and to serve humanity.

Earth is a place where we have free will to create our own experiences. This enables us to create a truly rewarding and fulfilling life, but also allows us to make mistakes and get ourselves into challenging situations. It is through demanding circumstances in our lives that we achieve the greatest learning.[6]

Before we come to earth, we plan each life carefully. We decide what lessons we want to learn, who we will be, and where we will be born. We choose the family that we will be born into and the other Souls who will accompany us and play specific roles in our upcoming life. Dr. Newton reported that there is a group of around one hundred other Souls whom we incarnate with in some of our multiple lifetimes, and a smaller group that we frequently include as part of our lives on earth.

We do not make these decisions about the life we will live by ourselves, as there are many other Souls involved in the planning process. We are all assigned a master guide at the time of our Soul birth and other guides to assist us. Each of us has a personal or primary guide who remains with us from the time we plan a new life until after we return home. We have a special loving relationship with these more advanced Souls who choose to be our guides. We are carefully matched with them to enhance our development.

Our primary guide is usually with us for multiple lifetimes or maybe even since we began incarnating on earth. This guide helps us plan each life and is there to assist us during our time on earth. When we incarnate on earth, we bring with us all the experiences of our past lives and our time in between lives in the spirit world.

INFLUENCES FROM PAST LIVES

Anything we have not resolved from a past life can be carried into our current life, including emotions, unresolved conflicts, and even physical influences from a past injury or deformity. For example, this can show up as an unexplained fear or sense of guilt, a birthmark, a physical deformity, or unexplained pain.

My first experience with physical influences that had an origin in a past life showing up in a current life occurred before I had obtained

---

6. Michael Newton Institute, Ann J. Clark, Karen Joy, Marilyn Hargreaves, and Joanne Selinske, *Wisdom of Souls* (Woodbury, MN: Llewellyn, 2019), 1, 2, 5.

training in past life regression. While I was completing graduate school, I obtained training in both therapeutic touch and Reiki, two therapeutic energy modalities that reduce stress and relieve pain. I offered energy work sessions to make extra money at that time. This is the experience I had with one of my patients.

Alan, a forty-three-year-old attorney, had been experiencing unexplained bouts of back pain that would practically incapacitate him for several days at a time, every year or so, for most of his life. As he became older, his symptoms started occurring every few months and were becoming worse. Over the years, he had undergone multiple examinations and many different tests. The traditional drug and physical therapies were not effective in relieving his discomfort. No physical cause had ever been found for these episodes.

The one thing that helped Alan was energy work, and I saw him each time he had an episode of back pain for about two years. These sessions were remarkably effective in relieving his pain. The last time I saw him, something unusual happened during the session.

While I was giving Alan energy work, he started talking about a battle. At first I asked him what he was talking about, but then, because he seemed so absorbed in what he was describing, I asked him to tell me about it. He described a battle with horses and wooden lances and expressed fear that they were losing the battle. He had become separated from his group and was being chased. Fascinated, I asked him to tell me what happened next. He described being knocked off his horse and landing on his back on a pile of jagged rocks. He started writhing in pain and said he could not move. He seemed to be in anguish.

I thought he might be remembering a movie he had seen and reassured him that he was just watching what was happening there. I reminded him that he was safe here with me. It took some time, but he calmed down and the pain disappeared.

I heard from Alan a year later. He had good news. He had spent a lot of quiet time recalling the battle experience and remembered many

more details and had come to believe that he was recalling a past life.
The fear he had felt back then mirrored some anxiety that had plagued
him in his current life, and he went to a counselor to help him deal with
his emotions. He had not had another episode of back pain since he had
last been in to see me.

I learned from this episode that we can carry anything we do not resolve into future lives. Remembering that experience, I realized that I must resolve my grief over losing my daughter, as I did not want to carry it forward into another life.

THE GUIDANCE AVAILABLE TO US

When we are born, our Soul joins with a human body and brain using the ego, or conscious self, to interact and live life on earth. A portion of our Soul energy always remains in the spirit world. The portion of our Soul energy that we bring into an incarnation becomes our Higher Self and is always communicating with us in the background, giving us guidance. As agreed, we forget that we are a Soul and see our physical existence is all there is.

Our guide knows us very well and is aware of the learning and development we hope to attain during our time on earth. The guide also knows about the other Souls that we have recruited to play supporting roles in our life and is able to see how our plans unfold. Our experiences on earth may not turn out as we planned, as we have free will and may not stick to our plans. Others in our life also have free will and may not follow the plans either.

However, we have help available should we need it. While we are living on earth, we have loving assistance and encouragement from our guides, angels, ancestors, departed loved ones, and wise elders in the spirit world. We are also able to connect with our Higher Self to receive guidance. Yet we may not take advantage of all this assistance, because due to our amnesia regarding our Soul home and who we really are, we may not realize that this help is always available.

As part of the planning process, we have ample opportunity to discuss our upcoming life with our Soul family and other Soul groups of which we are a part. Dr. Newton found that each Soul is created alongside other Souls, and this forms our Soul family. There may be one or more Soul families closely aligned with ours that we interact with regularly. We are also generally part of one or more other Soul groups based on our interests, what we are studying, and the work that we do in the spirit world. All these other Souls can help us choose the next life we will be living on earth, but the final choice is ours.

When we return home to the spirit world, our guide helps us review the life we just lived, the learning we achieved or failed to attain, and what our next steps should be in order to continue our evolution. More than one of our guides and wise elders may be involved in this process.

We plan each life to enable us to have experiences and learn lessons that allow us to grow spiritually. As our planned experiences and challenges unfold in our current life, we have many opportunities to build our Soul character. One of the experiences that helps us evolve is loss. When we have ambitious plans for Soul growth, we may plan for a loss. All losses help us grow, but great loss offers us an even greater opportunity to advance on our journey to enlightenment. We will discuss great loss and how it differs from other losses in the next chapter.

EXERCISE

PONDER YOUR BELIEFS ABOUT LIFE AND DEATH

In your notebook, record your thoughts about who we are as Souls and life on earth as presented in this chapter.

- How does your view of life compare with that presented in this chapter?
- Was any of this information new to you?
- Did you find anything that you do not agree with or find confusing?
- Does this information change your perspective on the meaning of life on earth? If so, how?

WHAT IS GREAT LOSS?

Great loss is an event that signals the end of a phase in our lives and a profound change in our life circumstances. It is losing someone or something that greatly upsets our world. It could be the loss of the emotional security of loving someone and being the one special person whom someone else loves. It might be the loss of what we view as our protection against some future eventuality, such as aging or potential misfortune. Perhaps we have lost the health and strength we have always counted on. Or it could be a loss producing a disillusioned feeling of all efforts coming to nothing, a lack of what it takes.

Our loss may have ejected us from a comfortable or consuming, distracted life in which we were not attending to our spiritual purpose as an incarnated Soul. Whatever the loss, there is a panicky feeling that we have lost our sense of certainty and security for the future.

Great loss takes something away from us that has been central in our lives. It is losing what has become so important to us that we have lost touch with who we really are. We may have made someone or something into what guides our daily life. Or, if we have been living life on the surface, having found a niche and a routine that allows us to avoid going any deeper into life, then this loss has ejected us from this comfortable hiding place. In either case, we have lost our focal point. Thus, this loss is a devastating, crushing blow.

We are not prepared to deal with this crisis, because when it happens, we are not connected to our inner guidance. The loss is a shock point in our lives that jolts us completely out of our comfort zone. No wonder we have such a hard time getting over it.

GREAT LOSS AS A SPIRITUAL EXPERIENCE

Great loss, as presented in this book, is a spiritual experience agreed to by us, as Souls, to give us time to pause and reflect on where our life is going. It occurs when we are disconnected from the guidance that our Higher Self can provide to us. The loss gives us a chance to return to our hopes and dreams for this lifetime. It is not a psychological disorder, even though it hits us harder and the pain lasts longer than it did for other losses we may have experienced.

Mental health professionals might see our reaction to great loss as prolonged grief disorder, a malady that affects an estimated one in ten bereaved people. Prolonged grief disorder is a syndrome with a distinct set of symptoms following the death of a loved one. The affected person is incapacitated by grief, feels devalued, and is in constant turmoil. It is characterized by an inability to adjust to life without the lost loved one.

Great loss is distinct from this syndrome for two reasons. First, those of us coping with great loss can function if not ideally, then at least adequately, in our daily lives. Second, we are not in constant turmoil, obsessing about our lost loved one, but rather we feel empty and uncertain in the wake of our loss. For us, it is a noteworthy spiritual experience that we can use to return to what we came to earth to accomplish.

Viewing the loss as a spiritual event enables us to approach it from a different perspective. The Soul sees the loss as an opportunity, not a disorder. If you are experiencing serious depression and/or having difficulty coping with daily life, I recommend that you seek professional assistance.

However, most of us continue to function in our daily lives, having passed through the acute phase of grieving, but need more time to heal from the havoc that such a significant loss has wrought in our lives.

While great loss may look like any other unfortunate loss from the outside, there are some unique aspects to this type of loss. There are some common reactions to any significant loss. What differentiates a great loss from other losses is the underlying feeling of emptiness, disenchantment, and aloneness that lingers long after the shock and the common emotional reactions related to the loss have passed.

The loss ends our daily life as it was and gives us a chance to see who we really are under all the distractions and misdirected outer focus. It is an opportunity to experience how we truly feel inside. Generally, we are deeply despondent over the nonfulfillment of our hopes and dreams. This happens because while we were either outer-focused or just floating on the surface of life, we were not making any progress in meeting our Soul objectives. While it may seem as if this disappointment comes from our loss, it really comes from what our loss has uncovered.

Over time, a great loss becomes less about who or what we have lost and more about what is missing in us. It is a loud knock on our door in the middle of the night that rudely awakens us and ejects us from the limiting patterns in which we have become stuck or from our comfortable existence living on the surface of life. This is not a time to hit the snooze button. Born of the love that our Higher Self has for our conscious human self, we have been given the gift of a time-out so that we can make our earth existence more purposeful, fulfilling, and joyous. However, we must make the effort to reach for a better life.

Nora, a friend of mine, did just that. She experienced a loss of safety and security from an unexpected crisis but eventually went on to make a new life for herself.

Nora had just come out of an ill-fated marriage that she had entered during her senior year in high school. She knew it was a mistake almost from the beginning, but became pregnant and decided she would try to stick it out. She barely managed to graduate before her pregnancy became obvious. Things continued to go downhill, and she fled several months later with her newborn daughter, ending the disastrous marriage. Her dysfunctional family provided no help, but she was able to secure public assistance. She daydreamed about someone coming along to rescue her.

On one rare night when she had a babysitter and could go out with some friends, she met "him." She describes how the minute he walked in the door of the bar, she knew he was the one. She had never felt this way before. He approached her right away, and they spent the night talking. After dating for only a few months, they were married, and she describes herself as drunk with happiness during those first few years, as she was so in love. She gave birth to two sons in rapid succession and was completely consumed with motherhood and homemaking. Her most important role during this time, though, was that of wife. She describes how she was so tuned in to her husband that when he had a good day, she had a good day. She was proud of how well she understood him and how in sync with him she was. Her marriage, home, and family became her life, and she abandoned any aspirations she once had.

Nora was shocked and devastated when her husband left her for someone else with what she experienced as little warning. She was left with three young children, no marketable skills, and a huge broken heart. She struggled the first couple of years to hold everything together, becoming seriously ill more than once. Sometime during this chaotic period, she discovered an inner strength that she had not realized she possessed. She spent quiet time reflecting on what she wanted in her life and decided that she would be the one to make it happen. She dropped the fantasy that someone would rescue her. She found a way to go back to school, developed a career in the helping professions, and eventually remarried.

A great loss is not the only kind of significant loss that we may experience in our lives, as we may be connected to our inner guidance when we experience a devastating loss. With this connection in place, coping with the loss will be a much different experience. A great loss occurs when we are not connected to our inner guidance, and thus it is a distinctive experience.

Great loss is unique because of (a) the attitudes and behaviors leading up to the loss, (b) the state we are in when the loss occurs, (c) the condition we find ourselves in after the loss, (d) the associated losses, and (e) the opportunity it provides for us to free ourselves from limiting patterns in our life or to dive deeper into life.

ATTITUDES AND BEHAVIORS BEFORE THE LOSS

The groundwork for a great loss is laid long before the actual loss occurs. During the period leading up to our loss, we are either stuck in patterns that limit our Soul growth or blindly unaware of the Soul's imperative for growth. Despite repeated urgings from our Higher Self (the part of our Soul energy that we bring into each incarnation) and the attempts of our guides to remind us why we are here on earth, we make no progress in addressing our life goals or expressing our true self. Either we have gradually lost our direction in life, as we become more and more attached to someone or something outside of ourselves, or we continue to live on the surface, letting life happen to us rather than through us.

We have a purpose for each life we live on earth. The purpose we choose and the lessons we select to learn are intended to move us toward enlightenment. Examples are loving unconditionally and developing tolerance, patience, or compassion. Each time we incarnate, we become a unique individual with special opportunities to express our distinctive strengths and talents. This allows us not only to advance spiritually through building our Soul character but also to live a satisfying and fulfilling life and make the world a better place.

Loving a child, spouse, parent, or friend dearly is among the joys of life on earth. Being part of a family and caring for others is a major source of fulfillment for many and an important service to others. Likewise, making a business, a career, a special ability or talent, physical skills, a place, or a charitable or other cause a major life focus can be very satisfying personally and constructive for society as well. Any one of these activities could serve as a vehicle to allow us to fulfill our life purpose. It does not matter what our occupation or social roles might be, because any of these pursuits will provide ample opportunity for us to acquire the attributes that make up our life purpose.

We can develop patience through caring for a child with special needs or through some form of exacting creative work. We can develop compassion through experiencing and recovering from abuse or through living a life of service. Before our incarnation, we plan the life circumstances, roles, and relationships that we believe will be most advantageous for us to fulfill our life purpose and have the experiences that we desire. The life situation we choose also gives us special opportunities to contribute to the world by expressing who we truly are as a Soul.

We agree to amnesia regarding who we are and what our purpose in coming to earth is before we incarnate so that we can fully engage in life and gain the most from our life experiences. It would hardly be the same challenge and allow us to develop our Soul character if we knew what was going on.

Thus, we enter each life as if it were a new experience and view our life circumstances and roles as all there is, being largely unaware of who we really are. We interact with the world through our ego, or conscious self, and forget about the portion of our Soul self that resides within us as our Higher Self.

However, it is the inner guidance from our Higher Self that enables us to stay on track during our earth life. This is the portion of our Soul energy that we bring with us to accomplish our mission. Among my patients, this is usually about 60 to 80 percent of their Soul energy. The remainder of our Soul energy remains in the spirit world.

Our Higher Self is constantly broadcasting messages to us. When we are awake, this information comes to us through our intuition, thoughts, emotions, and serendipitous experiences. When we are asleep, it comes through our dreams. These messages are subtle and easy to miss, but our Higher Self never stops trying to get our attention. If we live our life in a manner that allows us to be in the present moment and are not distracted by all the activity going on around us, it is easier to hear these messages.

The other resource that helps us move toward fulfilling our life purpose is the spiritual assistance that is always available to us while we are incarnated. Our personal guide is with us all the time, and we may have other guides to assist us during various phases of our life. Our guides know all about the plans that we have made for our current life. They try to gently steer us into staying on our life path by speaking to us in dreams, through synchronicities in our waking life, or even through the words of others. They are infinitely patient and continue to try to raise our awareness, but they never tell us what to do or make decisions for us.

We also have access to the wisdom and assistance of wise beings and angels when we call upon them. Our ancestors and departed loved ones watch over us and send us love and encouragement. However, we may not be aware of all these resources and thus may be unable to benefit directly from their existence. We may feel that we are alone and operating completely on our own. Nevertheless, these rich resources are operating in the background of our lives, helping us in unseen ways.

We have the option of building into the plans we make for each lifetime a set of contingencies that might be set into motion should we get off track and stop making progress on our spiritual goals. We do this when we intend to make significant spiritual progress during an incarnation. These contingent events have the potential to jolt us out of our limiting patterns and enable us to get back to spiritual growth and a more fulfilling life through a connection with our inner guidance. Great loss is one of those contingent events. The form it takes depends on our life circumstances at the time we need it and is not planned as a specific event.

Some individuals do naturally develop a relationship with their Higher Self and benefit greatly from listening to their inner guidance.

Others may come to discover and value this inner guidance through difficult experiences. When we fail to attend to our inner guidance, however, we become vulnerable to drifting off course in achieving the goals we have set for this lifetime, making little or no progress or becoming stuck in patterns that limit our spiritual growth.

Before great loss occurs, we are disconnected from our inner guidance and not making much progress toward the goals we have set for this lifetime. We may be either distracted and sleepwalking through life or focused on someone or something outside of ourselves.

Some of the ways we may become disconnected from our own life path include (a) blindly doing what we think we are supposed to be doing, (b) following the direction others think we should take, (c) acting out of an overdeveloped sense of responsibility or a sense of guilt, at the expense of our own self-development, and (d) choosing to live life at a superficial level.

These practices may temporarily make us feel that our life is headed in the right direction. However, as we move further away from our own hopes and dreams, as reflected in our inner guidance, we experience a growing emptiness and are not able to fully engage with life.

STATE OF MIND WHEN THE LOSS OCCURS

As the feeling of emptiness grows, we long for greater satisfaction and contentment in our lives. Our spiritual growth is limited at this point, and life is not very fulfilling. To ward off this yearning, we begin searching for something to bring us greater fulfillment. This is a time of vulnerability for us. It could be the trigger that allows us to connect to our inner guidance and proceed on a path to greater success and joy in our lives. However, if this is a life in which we have set the intention to make significant spiritual progress, we set the stage for great loss when we continue to ignore our inner guidance.

We may focus our attention even more strongly on someone or something outside of ourselves or become more distracted to make life more satisfying. Another direction we might take is to find someone or something new to focus on. This may be the reason behind a midlife crisis that leads to the ending of a long-term relationship, or the abandoning of a career for which we have made sacrifices in favor of someone or something new that we consider more exciting.

For a while, the excitement of something new in our life carries us. When we commit deeply to something outside of ourselves in this manner, it can feel like we have found a raft in the sea of life. We might conclude that we have found our calling or the role in life that we were meant to play. The something new might be a focus on the life of another person, such as a child or a lover. Or we may become consumed with the pursuit of a new career, some external achievement, or a goal such as being the best in the field or becoming wealthy or famous. If these new commitments coincide with the spiritual growth plans that we made for this life, then it is a win-win situation. However, when we are disconnected from our own inner guidance, we are not likely to use these activities to develop our Soul character.

We may create a life that is busy and distracted so that there is no time for self-reflection. Or we may settle for a comfortable lifestyle that we can maintain with little effort. This type of life can provide a haven for us, allowing us to avoid any self-reflection or struggle for growth.

However, as we become less aware of our inner guidance, we drift further away from fulfilling our life purpose. Over time, we can become stalled or stuck in patterns that block us from making progress on our own goals for this lifetime. We are ignoring our own inner compass. This is the state we are in when a great loss occurs. In hindsight, I can now see that I drifted off track in my own life through an overdeveloped sense of responsibility as a mother. When my daughter experienced the attack in which she was raped and robbed, I dropped everything to come to her assistance. Initially this was a good thing, as she needed my love and help. However, I carried it much too far, making her recovery the center of my life over a period of years, robbing both of us of the opportunity to forge our way down our own life paths.

As I look back, I recall a sense of fatigue and a growing sense of emptiness as I neglected my own self-care during that time. It was then that I could have taken some time for myself and developed a more balanced perspective. However, I chose instead to try even harder to help my daughter recover. A friend reminded me that during that time I told her that I felt as if I had found my mission in life in being there for my daughter when she needed me. When we are in a situation such as this, it is difficult to see what we are doing. Although denial is a normal reaction to circumstances that are out of our control, it serves as a roadblock to us facing the emotions that are created by the situation we find ourselves in. By suppressing these painful emotions, we fail to recognize the truth behind our thoughts, actions, and behaviors. I was suppressing the fear that I felt about my daughter never being able to make a successful recovery. Thus, I had no insight at the time about what was driving me to keep pushing so hard for her recovery.

While those close to me could see what was happening and were trying gently to get me to take more time for myself, I just could not see it at that time. I was juggling my practice, professional activities, and social activities, managing a household and a relationship with my romantic partner, and attending to my daughter's recovery. It was as if I was on a treadmill and someone kept increasing the speed. There was no time or space for listening to the inner promptings of my Higher Self. I kept thinking that if I just tried harder, things would work out. I believed that it was my responsibility as a mother to help my daughter find a way out of the situation in which she found herself.

What finally brought me to my senses was the information I received during a Life between Lives session, which I describe fully in chapter 11. Even then, I didn't absorb the information right away. There were two aspects of this session, so characteristic of communication from spirit, that enabled me to illuminate my blind spot. What allowed me to gain an understanding of my situation from this spiritual session was (a) the nonjudgmental approach and (b) the simplicity of the information.

When I listened to the recording of the session later at a time that I had set aside for self-reflection, the veracity of the guidance suddenly struck me. I was acting like a *fixer*, one who feels they can prevent suffering in others and show them the way to make things better. I was astonished that I had such a blind spot in my relationship with my daughter, as this had not been an issue for me in other areas of my life.

I had even previously taught in patient care about the dangers of being a fixer, doing for others what they should be doing for themselves. I had also worked with numerous patients who were exhausting themselves trying to fix someone in their lives. Their past life regressions and Life between Lives sessions had given them much the same advice that I had received in my session. Yet that was just the behavior I was exhibiting with my daughter.

Upon further reflection, I realized that I held some very unrealistic expectations about motherhood. Unconsciously, I felt that I should try to shield my daughter from life's traumatic and heartbreaking experiences and that it was my responsibility to show her how to fix them should they occur. I learned from my inner guidance that I was addressing the last vestiges of this behavior, which I had been working on for several lifetimes. Once I achieved this realization and began to work regularly with my inner guidance, I was able to let go of the last of my fixer tendencies. Yet I am also aware that I just might encounter another test in one of my closest relationships to see if I really have learned this lesson.

AFTER THE LOSS

When the great loss happens, it is as if the rug has been pulled out from under us, leaving us broken and shattered on the floor. The loss catches us in a state of disconnection from our inner guidance and from the help that is always available to us from the spirit realm. We have drifted away from our own hopes and dreams and have adopted those of others or have been just letting life shape us. Now, what we have invested in so heavily is gone, or our comfortable existence on the surface of life has been totally disrupted. This leaves us feeling lost and in deep despair.

Initially, after the loss, our feelings may seem like those experienced by most others who are grieving. However, after the early suffering has lightened, we feel worse instead of better. Even though we are the same person the morning after the loss, we may feel different right from the beginning. Some primal fears have been awakened in us.

We have gone from feeling as if we have finally found our mission in life, or a comfortable place to ride through it, to feeling that our worst fears have been realized. We have lost what made us feel safe, connected, worthy, and important. The worst thing that we can imagine has happened to us.

If we have lost a person, we may feel abandoned and all alone, even though we are surrounded by others. If we have lost money or possessions, we may feel unworthy or not good enough. If we have lost an important role or fallen short of an achievement we had been striving for, we may feel like a failure. If our busy, distracted life has suddenly come apart, we may feel blindsided.

Regardless of the nature of our loss, we may feel all these things or none of them. All we might feel is numb. What we have lost is our comfortable, safe place, or something that we had invested in so heavily that now we just do not feel in control of our life anymore.

ASSOCIATED LOSSES

There is more to mourn with a great loss than we initially realize, and that adds to the sense of emptiness we feel in its aftermath. In addition to what appears to be our main loss, we may also experience a loss of identity, expectations, security, and/or independence.

LOSS OF IDENTITY

After the death of my daughter, my only child, I experienced the loss of my identity as a mother. In the case of divorce, there is the loss of identity as a married person and the role of husband or wife. Other losses of identity that I have seen in my practice are those that occur when an individual leaves a religious group or an organization in which they have played a major role. In addition to a loss of faith or an activity that they have been passionate about, they also lose a sense of affiliation and community. A serious health problem can lead to a loss of identity as a strong, healthy individual. A lost job or career in which we were heavily invested can also lead to a loss of identity.

Loss of identity involves a lost sense of self, and that is something we must grieve. It is a feeling that we are no longer who we thought we were, and inevitably that leads to another question: Then who are we now? A loss of identity is especially difficult if we feel we had no control over the situation. Such was the case for Sophie.

Sophie, a fifty-eight-year-old physical therapist, really loved her work. She had been widowed several years earlier and had no children, so her work was her life. She owned her own therapy center and employed a small staff. She became remarkably close to her patients and enjoyed learning all about their lives. Sometimes former patients would call or write to let her know how they were doing. She was proud of the success of her practice and the way she was helping people.

While driving back from a trip to visit her brother and his family in another state, she was involved in a serious car accident and suffered several broken bones. Her staff was able to continue the practice as she recovered, but residual pain and some limitation in arm movement made her return to work difficult and painful. She struggled for several months trying to make it work, but finally had to concede that she no longer could practice.

Very reluctantly, she sold her practice and moved to her lake home. She hoped she would be able to recover further and return to work eventually. Unfortunately, she did not really gain enough improvement to do that and fell into a deep depression. Having put so much of herself into her career for so many years, she felt she no longer had any usefulness and did not know who she was anymore now that it was over.

I worked with Sophie on getting to know who she was apart from her professional role through journaling, meditation, and self-reflection.

These activities enabled her to remember the interests she had before beginning her professional life. She recalled a strong interest in journalism and writing. She took an online writing course and is now at work on her first novel.

LOSS OF EXPECTATIONS

A loss of expectations means that we must deal with some of our most cherished dreams going unfulfilled. With the death of my daughter, I lost all the expectations I had for the future, such as close family for mutual love and support, the possibility of grandchildren, and assistance in old age. This sense of loss often accompanies divorce or the death of a loved one such as a spouse, a child, a best friend, or some other treasured person in our lives. We can also experience it with failure to attain an achievement that we have worked hard for or with a stalled career trajectory.

When life does not go as we had envisioned, we feel a deep sense of grief and unfairness. We had a vision of how our lives would unfold and how we expected the world to operate. We feel disoriented when this happens because we believed that we understood how the world works and our assumptions have been violated.

LOSS OF SECURITY

A loss of security involves the loss of physical, emotional, mental, and spiritual well-being. Victims of violence or sexual or physical abuse lose their sense of safety. Jane, one of my patients, suffered losses from a robbery and an assault, and a lost sense of security was an associated loss.

Jane was robbed and sexually assaulted in a parking lot as she walked to her car after having dinner with friends. She was left lying on the asphalt, with her clothing in shreds, in an alley near where her car was parked. Her purse was gone, but on the sidewalk she found the keys that she had been clutching as she hurried to her car. She felt so ashamed and traumatized that instead of calling for help, she drove home and spent a long time in the shower trying to wash away the horror of the experience.

Later she reported the loss of her credit cards and an expensive ring, but was too ashamed and frightened to explain what had really happened to her. She had the locks changed in her apartment, went out only during the day, and slept with the lights on at night. The material things she had lost were secondary to her lost sense of security.

Jane came to see me for hypnotherapy sessions to reduce her anxiety. With her consent, I introduced her to a former patient of mine who was leading a rape survivors' group. The two became fast friends and are now working together to help other survivors of rape. Jane is no longer suffering from anxiety.

We expect to feel safe in our home, our community, and our relationships. When a spouse or romantic partner is unfaithful, we must grieve not only the betrayal but also the lost sense of safety in the relationship. A family who loses their home through foreclosure or eviction loses not only their place of residence but also their sense of security. They feel unstable and unprotected. This can lead to hypervigilance and a feeling of numbness. It is necessary to grieve the lost sense of security and learn to rebuild it.

LOSS OF INDEPENDENCE

Loss of independence occurs when we are no longer able to manage our own life and affairs. A health crisis that results in the loss of physical or cognitive abilities can compromise our independence. Our independence can also be affected when we lose a job or experience a financial setback, as we may need to rely on others for assistance.

Margaret, an eighty-six-year-old, became quite frail as she aged. When she fell and fractured her pelvis and hip, she became unable to care for herself. She had long been divorced, and her only son was deployed in a foreign country in military service. Although he was close to retirement, he was unable to be there to assist her through her convalescence. She was very sharp mentally and had been self-sufficient all her life. Her life had been peaceful, and she had been quite content before her fall. She confided that she had anticipated spending the remainder of her days just coasting along in this manner.

Fortunately, she was financially able to hire caregivers, but she became very depressed about not being able to do things for herself. I worked with her on adapting to her new circumstances and finding meaning in her life. She began by signing up for some classes and activities at the local senior center, allowing her caregiver to bring her to the site. She made several new friends and they started getting together at her house every week. Her mood improved significantly, and as her fractures healed, she regained her mobility and a limited ability to do things for herself.

She recently called to let me know that one of her new friends was planning to move in with her, providing her with companionship and additional assistance. She was excited about her son coming home soon and said that she had a new lease on life.

THE ENORMITY OF OUR LOSS

With great loss, we have lost much more than the someone or something that appears to others to be our loss. There is a primary loss and there may be one or more associated losses with which we must cope. We have lost our direction in life and we are devastated.

The good news is that we are no longer stalled and floating on the surface of life or stuck in a situation that was limiting our growth. We have been shocked awake. We now have the freedom and opportunity to get back on our own life path and live as our authentic self for the remainder of our days. This will allow us to reclaim joy and make the most of the time we have left here on earth.

That is not at all how the loss feels in the beginning. It is only further down the road from the initial pain that we can feel this potential freedom. And even after a beginning awareness of this potential dawns on us, we may feel that our loss was not a fair trade for this newfound freedom.

The loss is a shock that can push us to a new level of consciousness. Coming at a time when we are distracted and stalled in our spiritual growth, we have had a rude awakening. Losing what has been the center of our lives has a profound impact on us, causing our old attitudes and feelings to temporarily drop away. We now have an opportunity to rethink our anchors and search for new understandings. It is a time when we have an opportunity to recognize our strengths and reconnect with our Higher Self and spiritual guidance.

The great loss that we have experienced will not leave us the same. It forces us to acknowledge our vulnerabilities as well as our power. This crisis has a lesson embedded within it. It is an invitation to awaken to a greater reality and address the fears that dog us no matter how hard we try to leave them behind. Our fear of abandonment, not being good enough, or not belonging can be put to rest if we choose to accept this invitation for spiritual advancement.

AN OPPORTUNITY FOR GROWTH

During normal times, we tend not to go deeper. When things are going along as usual, whether we are busy and distracted or comfortably complacent, we are unlikely to engage in any Soul-searching. It is difficult to awaken to a higher consciousness when we are in our comfort zone. The great loss has knocked us out of our comfort zone. If we fail to use this opportunity to grow spiritually, we will suffer. If we do choose to grow, then this time provides an unparalleled opportunity for spiritual advancement. Accepting this invitation can lead us to living a joyous, fulfilling, fully engaged life after our loss. Next we will explore how the Soul views loss.

EXERCISE

REFLECT ON THE STATE OF YOUR LIFE BEFORE YOUR LOSS

Reflect on the state of your life prior to your loss and write about it in your notebook.

- What attitudes did you hold?
- Were you focused on the life of another person, a special project, or a quest?
- Was your life busy and distracted?
- Was your life comfortable but not challenging or exciting?

EXERCISE

IDENTIFY LOSSES ASSOCIATED WITH YOUR GREAT LOSS

Describe the loss or losses you have experienced along with your great loss, and write about your feelings regarding them in your notebook.

- Did you experience a loss of identity after your loss?
- Did you experience a loss of expectations?
- Did you experience a loss of security?
- Did you experience a loss of independence?

CHAPTER FOUR

GREAT LOSS FROM THE SOUL'S PERSPECTIVE

Rather than seeing great loss as a tragic occurrence, the Soul views it as a challenging opportunity. As Souls, we see loss as an ordeal that can help us learn and grow toward self-actualization. There is no loss in the spirit world, so that is one of the things that we come to earth to experience.

You are probably wondering at this point why anyone would ever choose such a thing. Well, it's because when we are still at home in the spirit world, we see loss differently than we do once we have come to earth and have experienced the amnesia of incarnation. As Souls, we seek such opportunities to develop different aspects of our Soul character. Our Soul identity is strengthened by living through and surviving loss. How we stand up to stressful experiences such as loss marks our progress in life.

Loss is one of the experiences that is already built into the earth school curriculum, and it touches each of us at some point in our lives. Unlike regular school, where we learn lessons and then are tested, in earth school we are given a test or challenge that teaches us a lesson. Loss is one of those challenging tests. As Souls, we may deliberately place ourselves in a situation that tests how we will react to loss. Of course, our conscious mind is unaware of this choice once we are living here on earth.

WHAT WE CAN LEARN FROM LOSS

All of us include loss in our life plans. One reason for this is because there is so much that we can learn from loss. We can learn these things in other ways as well, but loss in its varied forms often leads us to a different phase in our lives or into a whole new understanding of our current life situation. Thus, as Souls we seek the experience of loss for the opportunity it offers us for growth.

As Souls, we are aware that we are in school here on earth along with the other Souls who have agreed to join us during this incarnation. We all get together when we are preparing to come to earth and work out what roles we will play in each other's lives. Each of us makes our own plans for this life and sets intentions for what we want to learn. However, we agree to play complementary roles in each other's lives so that we can all advance spiritually. Often two or more Souls will come together to help each other have certain experiences that will help each of them grow.

Chances are that one or more of your current relationships are with Souls that you have incarnated with before. They may play the same role in your life as they did in one of your previous lives, or they may be in a different role this time. We agree to these plans before leaving the spirit realm. Loss or the potential for loss is often included in these plans.

Another reason we may include loss in our plans is to experience the emotions associated with grief. Encountering loss while living on earth allows us to experience powerful emotions. Experiencing these feelings is not possible when we are at home in the spirit world, because there we exist in universal harmony, peace, joy, and love. We come to earth to experience strong negative emotions and to learn from them. Loss teaches us about our emotions and encourages us to get to know ourselves better.

Through experiencing the powerful emotions of intense grief, we learn empathy and compassion for others going through difficult times. Through financial loss and failure, we learn humility and can exercise our ability to bounce back. The following are some things my patients have told me that they learned from experiencing a significant loss:

- I learned that life is precious, and it made me rethink my priorities. Grief shows you what is important.
- I came to realize that my husband was only a part of my life, not my whole life. I believe strongly that I will reunite with him when I die. In the meantime, I have a life to live while I am still here.
- I now feel greater compassion for others. My loss helped me see the blessings that are all around me.
- I learned through this experience that I am a lot stronger than I thought I was.
- I learned that I cannot control everything. I am more willing now to let things happen rather than try to make them happen.

KARMA

Karma is another reason we may choose to include loss in our life plans. The law of karma is not well understood and is often mistakenly seen as punishment, but the object is Soul development. If the Soul chooses one extreme, an opposite choice must be made at some point to even out Soul growth. For example, a Soul who has lived several lives in which they were very dependent on another person will choose opportunities to become more independent. Loss of a relationship may be a deliberate test to help us learn not to expect our happiness to be totally dependent on someone else.

LOSS OF A LOVED ONE

Almost everyone experiences the loss of someone they love, whether through death, divorce, abandonment, estrangement, or other circumstances. Facing the permanent end to a loving, nurturing relationship, or finally accepting that it will never be what we want it to be, can be an agonizing experience. Even though we know that all relationships are not permanent or may never develop in the way that we wish they would, it is still shocking when one of our important relationships, or the potential for one, ends. We experience strong emotions and intense grief. At the human level, we suffer.

The Soul, however, knows that relationships never truly end, as we are all eternally connected at the Soul level. The portion of our energy that is still present in the spirit world can welcome our lost loved ones back home. The portion of our being that becomes the Higher Self during our incarnations on earth still connects with the Soul of our lost loved one. Together they try to capture the awareness of our conscious self to let us know that our lost loved one is still with us, just in a different form.

In cases of divorce or estrangement, we continue to be connected as Souls and can communicate at this level while our body and conscious self sleeps. With the assistance of our Higher Self, we may come to a peaceful understanding of the situation. Reconciliation may not be possible during this incarnation on a conscious level, but we can still heal the wounds that the separation has caused for us and come to a peaceful resolution for ourselves. We can review the relationship to understand it better and then take action to complete it in a manner that promotes our spiritual growth. To do this we need to look at the relationship through the eyes of the Soul, or through the eyes of love.

The first action from this perspective is to shine a light on the situation to discover the whole truth. Ask yourself if you might have done something that hurt the other person. This is not a license to judge yourself, but rather an opportunity for you to complete the relationship in a compassionate manner, for both yourself and the other person. Sometimes an apology can be safely made, but often the apology should and must remain indirect. This may be hard to do if you feel you were mistreated and are the victim in the situation. From the Soul's perspective, however, full honesty is more important than being right.

OTHER LOSSES

Loss of a job, financial stability, a home, health, faith, independence, a beloved pet, or other major losses can have just as great of or an even greater impact on our lives than losing a loved one. Harold was devastated by the loss of a beloved pet.

Harold attended one of my Great Loss workshops. He had signed up, but then was going to back out because he thought others would not understand his loss and would think that he should not be there. I assured him that was not the case and encouraged him to attend, letting him know that he was not the first one to attend with a similar loss. Harold had lost his wife almost ten years earlier, and since they had no children, he now had no close family nearby.

Harold's work kept him busy, but when he retired, initially he felt lost. That was when he decided to adopt a pet. He described how it was the ugliest puppy in the pound that caught his eye. The others seemed so eager when he approached their cages, but this one just looked away. When the puppy realized he was being adopted, he was overjoyed and the two of them bonded immediately. He named the dog Tiny because he was so skinny, and he now laughs about how big Tiny has become. He says that Tiny grew big enough to fill all the empty spaces in his life and take away his loneliness. He confesses that his retirement made him feel that he had nothing left to live for.

While adopting Tiny made Harold feel less alone and gave him someone to care for, it also allowed him to live at a superficial level and avoid dealing with his feelings. They spent six years together and were inseparable.

One evening, on a late-night walk in an area he usually avoided, Harold was approached by two teenagers. One pointed a gun at him and demanded money. Tiny lunged at the gunman and was shot in midair. The dog slumped to the sidewalk, bleeding profusely, as the two teenagers ran away. A police car arrived shortly after, and they rushed Tiny to an emergency animal clinic. Unfortunately, Tiny died in Harold's arms before they arrived.

Harold was devastated and felt guilty about Tiny's death, but what was most difficult for him was dealing with all the memories of other losses that the incident triggered for him. The loss of his beloved pet shocked him out of the comfortable, superficial state in which he had been living, and his buried feelings came rushing out.

Harold used the tools introduced in the workshop to revisit unresolved feelings from his past. He expressed gratitude for the group's acceptance of the importance that the loss of a much-loved pet had for him. Facing this loss allowed him to heal unresolved feelings from the past and cleared the way for a better future for him. He advises others not to discount the importance that pets can have in our lives.

As Souls, we understand that when we incarnate and join with a human body, we will face earth's hardships as well as enjoy its advantages. This is one of the hard truths about being human. Both experiences provide opportunities for spiritual growth. However, it is the hardships that provide us with some of the best learning opportunities.

While our conscious self perceives this kind of loss as adversity, as a Soul we see events such as these as hopeful. That is because as we face the difficulties created by loss, we increase our ability to see the truth of who we really are. Such losses instill apprehension in our ego, or conscious self, but as a Soul we see them as an opportunity to transcend our fear by facing it and developing the strength to endure it.

Our ego panics when facing loss because it perceives that we no longer have security and stability. In contrast, as a Soul we are hopeful. This may be the time when we come to our senses. It may be a time when we reexamine our lives to evaluate how satisfied we really were before the loss. This loss may lead us to connect with our inner guidance or even to directly experience who we truly are.

ASSOCIATED LOSSES

One of the things that makes a great loss so difficult is that we lose more than what appears to be our primary loss. What we have lost can take away our sense of identity and steal our dreams for the future. We are left feeling alone and insecure. We are most vulnerable when we have been hurt.

Our response to the loss reveals our level of consciousness. If we respond with anger or bitterness, then we enter that level of consciousness. From the perspective of the Soul, this is a time for healing through establishing a strong connection between our Higher Self and our conscious self. It is also a time for showing love and compassion for ourselves and for others.

Having to give up a treasured career because of physical illness was a difficult experience for Ben. He experienced an onerous loss of identity and was left feeling very unstable. The accompanying loss of independence and shattering of future expectations left him in despair.

Ben, a forty-eight-year-old physician, had dreamed of being a doctor since he was a child. He spent long years in medical school, residency, and specialty training in oncology. Long hours in his office seeing patients and even longer days at the hospital took up most of his time. While the work was often exhausting, he loved what he was doing.

He began having weakness in his arms and hands that made it difficult for him to write and hold on to charts, and he often stumbled when walking through the halls of the hospital. These symptoms worsened, and he underwent an evaluation and a series of tests. Eventually he was diagnosed with amyotrophic lateral sclerosis (Lou Gehrig's disease) and, despite the latest treatments, was unable to continue his practice.

Ben had a difficult time accepting the diagnosis and an even harder time giving up his practice. The local university offered him a teaching position, but he wanted to practice, not teach. Not only did he lose his independence, but he lost all his dreams for the future as well. The task ahead of him was reformulating his identity.

Ben came to me for hypnotherapy sessions for anxiety and depression and then had a past life regression and a Life between Lives session. Following the advice of his guides received during these sessions, he started meditating. This was something he had always planned to do but had never actually made the time for. His dedication to his work had kept him so busy and distracted that he had never taken any time to get to know himself and explore how he felt about life.

While he was a bit skeptical about meditation, Ben did give it a try and started feeling less anxious after a couple of weeks. The next thing that happened was that he started thinking about why he had this illness, a question he had heard from so many of his patients. He began watching YouTube videos and documentaries on his computer. This led him to explore newer ideas about the nature of consciousness and the Soul. He started listening to audiobooks on philosophy and spirituality. While he still has a way to go in adjusting to his new circumstances and reformulating his identity, he is on his way.

When we lose something that has been a major part of our life, we are left wondering who we are. This loss of identity can be almost as difficult as recovering from what we have lost. Often this comes paired with the loss of a whole set of expectations and a feeling of instability. In Ben's case, it also involved a loss of independence. As a Soul, however, we see this as being the right set of circumstances for our conscious self to get to know who we truly are. It is a time for us to discover our hidden talents, appreciate our strengths, explore our desires, and embrace our true nature. Ben has started to do just that. A great loss is particularly painful because it comes at a time when we have been focused on someone or something outside of ourselves or are living life superficially and are not in touch with our inner guidance. Our Higher Self and those who love, protect, and guide us from the spiritual realm are aware of how difficult a time this is for us.

Our departed loved ones and our ancestors send us love and encouragement. While this is a sad and discouraging time for our conscious self, our Soul and spiritual helpers see this as a time for us to embrace our true self and get back on our spiritual path.

While we may not be aware of it, we receive special guidance, energy, and love to assist us in doing just that. We are given encouragement, hope, and serendipitous opportunities to move forward in a positive direction in our lives. However, we have free will, and the choice of how we proceed with our life after a great loss is left up to us.

THE SOUL'S VIEW OF GREAT LOSS

Our Soul views great loss as a course correction for our life. Course corrections provide excellent opportunities for development of Soul character and thus are desired by the Soul. We learn through experience and making mistakes or encountering obstacles to overcome. Difficult situations help us learn even more rapidly.

We can liken the guidance of our Higher Self, the portion of our Soul energy that we bring into each incarnation, to a GPS (Global Positioning System) in our car. It is there to help us find our way to our intended destination. Before we start on our trip, we set our destination, and the verbal directions of the GPS guide us on our way. Likewise, as Souls, we set a destination (purpose) for each lifetime and our Higher Self guides us on our way in life. Our Higher Self is there to guide us because the amnesia we experience when we incarnate means that we do not remember our purpose and what we hope to experience and learn.

Our Soul tries repeatedly to get through to our conscious self and alert us when we are going nowhere or are headed in the wrong direction. Messages from our Soul appear in symbols, metaphors, and feelings. By taking time for self-reflection and getting to know ourselves, we become better able to interpret these signals. Too many times, though, we run on autopilot or stay so busy, putting out one fire after another to keep things running smoothly, that we fail to pick up on these subtle cues. We can become stuck in this mode, blocking our ability to move forward with any of the plans we made for this lifetime.

From the Soul's perspective, when we are caught up in someone else's life or other people's dreams, we are not making progress toward the goals that we set for this lifetime. When we are complacent or distracted and not doing any self-reflection or Soul-searching, spiritual progress is stalled. Our spirit guides, Soul family, and wise beings from back home in the spirit world also try to help us see where we are stalled. They are aware of what we have planned for this lifetime and see when we are stuck in growth-limiting patterns.

It is only when our Soul cannot get through to our conscious self about how far we have drifted from our life purpose that something more powerful is needed. At this point what is required is something to help us get unstuck and go back to our own life path. We anticipated in our life planning that something like this might happen and made provisions for it through contingency plans. Contingency plans are more prominent in lifetimes in which we plan to achieve significant spiritual growth.

When our spiritual growth is blocked by patterns in our life, it is then that our Soul might agree to a contingency plan to resolve this dilemma. Great loss is a life shock that can enable us to break free from stalled patterns or limiting circumstances that have been holding us back.

The nature of the loss involved in this contingency plan is determined by our life situation at the time. For example, if we have become overly involved in the life of another person, letting their activities, needs, and emotions rule our days, then our loss will be associated with them. This may be the death of that person, as it was for me with the loss of my daughter. Or the loss may be a divorce, an estrangement, an encroachment of a third party in the relationship, a distant move, or anything that breaks that connection. If we become preoccupied with business success and financial gain, then the loss will be something that interrupts that quest.

Thus, from the Soul's perspective, great loss is a wake-up call, alerting our conscious self that we are not going anywhere. It is a traumatic event meant to assist us in getting back on our life path when we stall or drift too far off track. It is a contingency built into the earth curriculum to free us from situations in which we are blocked from making progress in our own life plan.

We can compare this situation to that of a car that gets stuck in the mud and is just spinning its wheels, sinking deeper and deeper into the mire, unable to move on to its destination. By the same token, we can get stuck in limiting patterns that keep us from the learning and growth that we came to earth to achieve. Getting stuck and needing a wake-up call is considered to be a fortuitous event by the Soul in its journey because of the potential it holds for Soul growth and spiritual advancement.

When we make plans for the life that we are about to live on earth, we build in contingency plans for just such an eventuality. Getting unstuck or getting started again when we are stalled is something that can help us move on. It enables us to make the most of the rest of our time on earth so that we can make this incarnation count.

SOUL EMOTIONS

At the Soul level, we are wise and loving. One of our most important qualities as a Soul is joy. Our Soul and spiritual helpers cheer for our conscious self to accept the invitation embedded in great loss to join with our Higher Self and become our fully integrated authentic self. This leads us to joy and fulfillment and allows us to achieve our life purpose.

The emotions of the Soul are deep. We lament the inability of our conscious self to realize when we are sacrificing our true nature to achieve career and financial success or by tethering our focus to the life of another. The Soul experiences how we may feel a deep loneliness inside as we drive for external achievement, even though we are surrounded by many others.

It saddens us, as Souls, to see our conscious self pursue those things that are transitory. Our lack of awareness of what is truly enduring disheartens the Soul. The Soul deplores our blindness to what can truly heal us. The Soul cherishes the emotions of loving kindness, because that restores us.

After a great loss, the time comes when we must make a choice about the direction that our life will take. This is a defining moment, a moment that can shape the rest of our lives. We will discuss defining moments and how to prepare for them next.

EXERCISE

LEARNING GAINED FROM LOSS

Discuss what you have learned from your great loss and record it in your notebook.

- What have you learned about yourself? Your strengths? Your values?
- What have you learned about life?
- What have you learned about your relationships?
- What have you learned about what is most important to you?
- What have you discovered about your hopes for the future?

CHAPTER FIVE

DEFINING MOMENTS

After a great loss, we eventually come to a point where we must face the choice of how to live out the rest of our lives. This is a defining moment for us. A defining moment is a point in time when we come to a fork in the road. It is a time when, depending on the moment and how we react to it, our lives could go in one direction or another.

Great loss is an experience that fundamentally changes us, but what that change turns out to be is up to us. How we react during the defining moment or moments that arise in the aftermath of our loss will determine the direction in which the rest of our life will go.

We do not get to choose the timing of our defining moments. They are like an open-book test in earth school, only we do not realize that we have been tested until it is over. We just need to stand and face these moments when they come, no matter what state we are in.

We all have defining moments in our lives that change the way we think and act. But no defining moments are as important as the ones that come after a shock, such as a great loss, that frees us from our stalled or limiting patterns. Great loss gives us an opportunity to set off in a new direction in our lives. We have little to no fear in boldly moving forward in our lives because what we feared the most has already happened to us.

The direction we choose to take is not nearly as important as connecting with our inner guidance to enable us to get back to the goals that we set for this lifetime. When we are in touch with our inner guidance, any situation we choose can be used to achieve our life purpose. Our Higher Self hopes that we will choose to heal by integrating our conscious self and Higher Self to become our authentic, or true, self as we live out the remainder of our days on earth. However, the choice is ours to make.

TIME LEADING UP TO OUR DEFINING MOMENTS

Loss that occurs when we are not in touch with our inner guidance is a crisis. Losing the someone or something that has become a major part of the life we have built by focusing outside of ourselves or being suddenly jolted from the comfortable place where we have been stalled and not making progress on our own life goals is a devastating loss. We are left in a confused and demoralized state and do not know what to do next.

Just when we need it the most, we are not in touch with our Higher Self and the spiritual guidance that could lead us toward healing. We do not know how to go on or even if we want to. We are not in the best place to face a new challenge, but that is just when it comes. It is during our darkest moments that we must gather our strength to focus and see the light.

There really is no warning before a defining moment comes, and we generally are not aware that it has occurred at all until much later. The direction that the decision we make in that split second takes us in does not become clear until we are further down the road. We can prepare for these defining moments, however. There are some early signs that we may be coming to a crossroads.

After we have passed through the typical initial reactions to loss, we move into a period where we feel numb and dead inside but anxious at the same time. While this may sound like depression, a more apt way to describe it, from a spiritual perspective, is a state of disconnection from our inner compass. We have not fully recovered from our loss, but the acute pain we felt previously is now replaced by feelings of insecurity and confusion. It is as if we have been set adrift without an anchor and feel like we are going either nowhere or perhaps to somewhere that we do not want to go. Being unaware of our inner guidance, we feel very unsettled.

We have not found anything yet to replace what we have lost. The resulting aimless state alternates with a sense of despair over what we have lost. We can put up with these feelings for just so long before we become restless and start to wonder just how long this uncomfortable situation is going to go on. This is a clue that a defining moment is coming, but it will go by so quickly that we probably will not even notice it. It usually takes some time to realize how important these moments are. But an awareness that they are coming can help us prepare for them.

THE CHOICE BEFORE US

Our conscious self comes to a breaking point with a sense of desperation, where we know we must move on. We have had just about enough of being in such an uneasy place. This alerts us that a defining moment is on the way. When it arrives, we will make a split-second decision. This decision made in the blink of an eye carries with it consequences that will shape our life following our loss.

We can either define this moment or let it define us. A recognition that a defining moment is coming can help us get ready for it. Since it is a moment that will shape us as a person, we can prepare for it by visualizing what we would like our future life to be.

Our loss does not define us. It is not what we have been through that defines us, but how we get through it. Getting through it is what brings us to life on the other side of our loss.

After a loss, we basically have just two choices: (1) move forward in our life with faith or power, or (2) step backward by doing nothing or making a choice that is not in our best interest. There are several ways that we might go in either of these directions.

SLIDING INTO ANGER AND BITTERNESS

After a loss, we could remain right where we are by not making a choice at all. This might work for a while, but discontent will grow. We cannot really stay in this uncomfortable state of limbo, and if we do not do something about it, we will slide into anger and bitterness. Bitterness springs from a combination of fear and disappointment. If we allow these feelings to grow, they can become hardened and strongly affect the quality of our life.

When we are feeling bitter, we can no longer enjoy the good things in life. We see wrongdoing everywhere and become cynical. In this state we become blind to the good things in our life. Bitterness is the residue that unresolved anger leaves behind. This keeps us attached to the very thing that is creating our discomfort. Bella came to see me for help in coping with the stress she was feeling over her sudden and unwelcome retirement. She was unable to let go of the anger she felt over the loss of a job that she loved.

> Bella complained that she had been feeling angry and depressed since she left her job. She had been with the same Fortune 500 company for thirty years and had worked her way up to becoming a special associate of the chief executive officer (CEO) in her public relations role. Through her close association with her boss, the CEO, she had been involved with many of the major activities of the corporation.
>
> Bella developed a close working relationship with her boss and described herself as an "office wife." Both he and his wife saw her in this capacity and included her in many of their social activities. Having divorced many years earlier, Bella's work and work-related associations became her life. All was well until her boss had a heart attack. He survived but chose to resign from the company. An associate whom

Bella got along well with took over for him temporarily, but the working relationship was just not the same. She no longer felt special.

The trouble really began, however, when the company hired a new CEO. Bella had expected to work closely with him as well, but they did not get along. Many in the former executive group were fired, but because of her age, she was forced to retire. This exasperated her, and she did not leave quietly. She let everyone around her know how unfairly she was being treated and even tried to sue the company for age discrimination. Now out of options, Bella's anger continued to fester, and she declared that she felt like a nobody.

Bella did a past life regression and went back to a life in the past where she had experienced a similar situation. Her guides gave her many gentle suggestions about seeing the current situation from a different perspective and exploring new opportunities in her life. Her response to the session was defensive, and she stated that the advice just did not fit her.

She does have a recording of the session and some questions designed to trigger self-reflection. It is not unusual for patients to take some time before they can absorb the wisdom from one of these sessions. The seeds have been planted, and I know that spirit will continue to encourage her to benefit from this life experience.

Feeling bitter toward the people or circumstances in our life can become toxic over time. It can creep into many aspects of life. However, it is never too late to change and do something to correct it. Just because the person we loved is gone or a weighty disappointment occurred in the past does not mean good things are not in store for us in the future.

There most likely is a lesson we can benefit from in the experience that can help us move forward. We will address moving out of anger and bitterness in the next chapter.

LOSING OURSELVES IN ADDICTION

Another way to avoid making a choice about living after loss is to block the intense emotional pain of grieving with drugs or alcohol. Because the pain of grieving is so intense, there is a natural tendency to want to avoid it. Turning to alcohol or drugs may hide the pain or allow us to push it away, but it does not heal the pain. Using substances as solace for the powerful feelings that accompany loss too often can lead to addiction and compound the problem.

BECOMING STALLED OR STUCK AGAIN

Another way to step backward is to (a) find a new person or thing outside of ourselves to focus upon, or (b) become very busy and distracted so that we can avoid our deeper feelings and continue to live on the surface of life. These moves allow us to bury our pain but also prevent us from connecting with our inner guidance and the spiritual support that is available to us.

This may temporarily feel like recovery, because the pain goes away and the excitement of something new in our life creates a renewed sense of well-being. However, since we have not completely dealt with the pain of our loss and are not connected to our inner guidance, it is only a matter of time before we end up back where we were before our great loss. I allowed myself to get excessively busy for a short period after my loss, until I saw that I was just avoiding my pain.

QUICKLY FINDING A NEW RELATIONSHIP

Losing a loved one through death or suffering the end of a relationship with a difficult breakup or divorce can leave a marked void in our lives. It is tempting to think that jumping into a new relationship will allow faster healing from the old one, but rarely does that work.

The gift of a great loss is freedom from the patterns in the previous relationship that were limiting our growth. Getting right back into a new relationship is like trying to cover up a wound without healing it first. Getting involved in a new relationship too soon precludes us from learning anything from the past relationship and blocks a connection with our inner guidance. It is likely that we will repeat the same patterns under new circumstances.

Jill, an attractive thirty-seven-year-old woman, had gone through a long, difficult divorce and was tired of being alone. Even before the divorce had been finalized, she joined several online dating sites hoping to find a new relationship. She received a lot of attention from men on these sites and arranged to meet several of them. This proved to be quite frustrating, as either she just was not attracted to them or she was attracted to them but after one or two dates they never called her back. Meanwhile she was feeling sadder and more alone than ever. This prompted her to attend one of my Great Loss workshops. She realized that she had not dealt adequately with her grief over losing her marriage, even though so much time had already passed. Jill focused on healing her feelings of abandonment, engaging in self-care, and visualizing what she wanted in a new relationship.

Becoming involved with another cause or quest without taking time for self-reflection and recovery is another way to take a step backward. Great loss offers us an opportunity to get back into balance in our lives. When we are driven to achieve more than is necessary, we miss the enjoyment of the present moment and put off pleasure to some distant future. Pushing ourselves to the point of exhaustion or to the exclusion of important people in our lives robs us of our joy.

Through connecting with our inner guidance, we can remember the plans and goals we set before incarnating here on earth. This connection nourishes us and allows our priorities to shift from chasing after an elusive satisfaction to being fully present in the moment, open to both inner and spiritual guidance. Getting involved in a consuming quest or cause again too quickly does not give us the opportunity to retrieve our forgotten hopes and dreams.

RETURNING TO DISTRACTED LIVING

Sliding back into distracted living can also be a step backward. Distracted living is when we miss out on much of life because we are not paying attention. Distractions take precious time away from us and make us lose our sense of direction. We are not connected to our inner guidance when we are distracted, which impedes our progress toward our goals and dreams. This makes us miss opportunities in life.

Distracted living is a form of living life on a superficial level, without taking the time to deal with what is going on inside. Deeper difficulties remain hidden inside as we move from one scene of life to another. We skate on the surface of life without being in touch with our core.

The more we become engrossed in our daily routine, the more our thoughts tend to become reactions to what is going on outside of us. What happens on the outside is not under our control, and our lives tend to move in an unfocused way instead of with purpose. As time progresses, shallowness tends to develop, taking us further away from our inner guidance and greater purpose in life. Life on the surface can seem easier, but that is not why, as a Soul, we chose to come here.

There are many distractions available to us that can keep us from connecting with our feelings or hearing the quiet voice of our Higher Self. We can watch mindless television, spend hours on the computer with email and social media, or play games on our phone. These activities keep boredom at bay and protect us from our emotions that are simmering just under the surface. But the clock keeps on ticking and our limited time here on earth is passing by without us making any progress.

The antidote to distracted living is to slow down and reflect on what is really important to us. Then we need to act to make time for those things in our busy life. A connection with our Higher Self will help us do this.

MOVING FORWARD WITH FAITH AND POWER

The gift of great loss is that we have been freed from stalled or limiting patterns in our life that were keeping us from making progress on the spiritual goals that we set as Souls before incarnating here on earth. Thus, the way forward is to connect with that portion of our Soul self that we carry within, our Higher Self. This will enable us to receive inner guidance that will take us in the direction that our Soul self intended for this lifetime.

Connecting with our inner guidance may seem like an extremely difficult thing to do at first. Nonetheless, we can hold an intention for the life that we hope to have in the future as we fully heal from our great loss. Then, when we experience a defining moment, we will be prepared to make a choice that will carry us in that direction.

We will cover connecting with our Higher Self more fully in chapter 8. When we follow our inner guidance, healing after a great loss will lead us down a different path, one that will make us stronger and happier.

This is a time to get to know our authentic self. We grow into our authentic self when we allow our conscious self (ego) and our inner self (Higher Self) to align. A connection with our inner guidance and an acceptance of the spiritual assistance that is always available to us will lead us down the right path, the one that is exactly right for us. I honestly believe that when one door closes, another opens. We can find a new purpose and renewed passion in our lives at any age. Facing my great loss in my seventies has convinced me of that!

> *Lorraine lost her husband of over sixty years at the age of eighty-four. Her children wanted her to move into assisted living, even though she looked and acted much younger than her years and was vibrantly healthy. Instead, she enrolled in one of my Great Loss workshops, determined to heal and move on with her life. She was an inspiration to all of us. She did decide to sell the big house in which she and her husband had been living but rejected the idea of moving into assisted living. She is now leading a peaceful, happy life in a new apartment and volunteering at a food bank.*

YOU CAN HAVE A CHANGE OF HEART

Do not stress over the defining moments that come after your loss. Should you make a choice that is not in your best interest, you can always change course. Sometime down the road, you will have a moment of clarity where you will know whether you are on the right track.

I chose to jump right back into my professional activities full force before I had fully healed from my great loss. I set up a schedule for myself that allowed me to forget about my loss and the pain I still carried from it. That worked for a short while, but I became exhausted and started to feel incredibly sad again. I cut back on my activities as I realized that I had not fully healed.

Grief allows us to survive losses by immersing us in a state that is set apart from everyday life. If we cannot move fully into our grief, we will either (a) experience destabilization in our lives, (b) waste a lot of time and energy by focusing on someone or something else outside of ourselves, or (c) distract ourselves by diving back into busy, superficial living. What we need to do is slow down, turn inward, embrace our feelings, and accept support.

I slowed down, attempted to become centered and grounded, and concentrated on fully experiencing my feelings. After some reflection, I chose to join a grief recovery group, which proved to be immensely helpful. From there I went on to restructure my professional activities in a way that was much more personally satisfying to me.

In the next several chapters, we will discuss specific strategies for healing from great loss. I will also share some of the other steps I took in healing from my loss and finding joy again. For me, each step was necessary, and I found that my connection with my inner guidance was strengthened as I made my way through each one. Your journey may be different, and as your connection to your inner guidance becomes stronger, you will be guided toward just the healing practices that you need. We all grieve in our own way and in our own time, but we can support each other as we each make our way to healing.

Here are some ways to prepare for the defining moments that follow a great loss:

- Slow down and allow yourself to feel the sadness.
- Make time for self-reflection and write about your feelings.
- Visualize what you would like your life to be in your new circumstances.
- Consider joining a grief recovery group.

Know that should you make a choice that down the road doesn't feel right, you can always change direction.

EXERCISE

VISUALIZE WHAT YOU WOULD LIKE YOUR FUTURE TO BE

Take some time to reflect on how you would like your life to be in the future. This can be anything you would like it to be. See yourself in various scenes in this life in the future. Record your vision in your notebook.

CHAPTER SIX

COPING WITH THE PHYSICAL AFTERMATH OF GREAT LOSS

As a Soul, we value loss because of the opportunity it affords us for spiritual advancement. The human part of us, however, finds loss and the grief that follows to be a very distressing experience. In the case of a great loss, our entire being is involved in the anguish we feel and in the adjustment to the changed circumstances of our lives. We experience prolonged stress as we struggle to adjust, and this is likely to lead to some physical consequences.

Things just are not the same after a serious loss. Thus, when we experience a significant loss, we must relearn how to live our lives. We need to learn new ways to take care of ourselves in the changed situation that we find ourselves in.

I had experienced painful losses before my great loss. Thus, I was familiar with the emotional, physical, and spiritual ramifications of loss that are described in the many excellent books available on loss and grieving. The loss of my daughter, however, was my first great loss, a loss that significantly changed the circumstances of my life. Nothing I had read prepared me for the longer-term effects of such a shock.

THE CONNECTION BETWEEN BODY AND SOUL

We have learned from Dr. Newton's work that during our life on earth, the Soul and the body are inseparably intertwined. In his 2000 book *Destiny of Souls*, he explains that the Soul-body partnership really begins in the fetus, where the Soul and the brain of the new baby become one mind. Thus, as Souls, we become a unified entity with an ego, or conscious self, to allow us to navigate everyday life in our human body.

Our body and mind share a common chemical language and are constantly communicating with each other. Thus, great loss creates a turmoil that affects both our mind and our body, and we must tend to each of these areas as we heal from our loss.

The portion of our Soul energy that we bring into this incarnation resides within us as our Higher Self. Our Higher Self knows that despite the benefits for Soul development, our loss will be difficult for us to bear psychologically and our body will be affected as well. Our Higher Self stands ready to help us become aware of our strength and resilience and to assist us through this difficult time.

Our guides, angels, and wise beings are always available to give us assistance. All we need to do is call upon them. Our ancestors and departed loved ones are sending us love and encouragement. However, our conscious self is overwhelmed at this time and largely unaware of this higher perspective and the inner guidance available to help us through this distressing time.

THE LONG-TERM EFFECTS OF GREAT LOSS

Because of the enormity of the loss and the extended time it takes for recuperation, it is likely that we will experience some physical aftereffects as we strive to adjust to our loss. Grieving is a process that is different for everyone, and there is no normal progression. What each of us experiences in loss and its aftermath is unique to us. However, healing from great loss generally takes longer and is more complex than with other losses. There are many parts of the great loss experience that are unexpected and unexplained. There are parts of the grieving process that we must deal with long after our loss has taken place.

When we first learn of our loss, our emotional well-being feels threatened and we go into shock. Our body prepares for fight or flight and our autonomic nervous system is thrust into overdrive. A slew of catecholamines, or stress hormones, are released into the bloodstream by the adrenal glands. These include dopamine, norepinephrine, and adrenaline. Corticosteroids and stress hormones flood our system, and we are made ready for survival. This response is particularly useful if we are being physically threatened but is not beneficial or adaptive in the long term.

It is this reaction that gives rise to the physical symptoms that commonly occur following the loss of a loved one, which are described in detail in the many grief resources available. This reaction can occur with any significant loss. Most of us probably experienced many of these physical effects earlier in response to our loss. We may have experienced fatigue, random aches and pains, restlessness, gastric distress, heart palpitations, shortness of breath, either loss of appetite or indulgence in comfort food, difficulty sleeping, and/or muscle weakness.

One of the substances released when we are stressed is cortisol. This hormone is important for our bodies to function normally, but too much cortisol can be bad for our health. When cortisol levels stay too high for too long, as they are likely to do after a great loss, we can experience a range of unwanted symptoms. Lowered immunity and inflammatory responses are common consequences. This can show up as a cold or sore throat, aches and pains, and perhaps a flare-up of a chronic disease we may have, such as arthritis or fibromyalgia.

For most losses, the stress lessens, and these symptoms subside in a few months to a year. However, with great loss, the stress may be longer term, and cortisol levels can remain elevated. Thus, the consequences are more serious. There are several possibilities that we need to consider in our self-care and physical recovery.

HEIGHTENED SUSCEPTIBILITY TO ILLNESS

Because prolonged stress following a great loss weakens our immune system, we become more susceptible to illness. An elevated level of cortisol can occur not just from the stress of loss but also from a lack of sleep and depression, common occurrences after a great loss. This affects the thymus gland, causing it to malfunction and be unable to produce adequate effective white blood cells to protect us from bacteria, viruses, or even precancerous cells, thus making us more susceptible to infection.

In the first year following the death of my daughter, I developed severe bronchitis, and in the second year, I developed viral pneumonia, which required hospitalization. I was dismayed, because as a nurse, I have always been very health-conscious and I used to rarely even catch a cold. However, I had to acknowledge that I had not been eating well, sleeping enough, or getting much exercise. We may neglect our self-care while we are mourning our loss, and that makes us even more prone to coming down with an illness.

Most bereaved people experience a minor physical illness in the first four to six months after the death of their loved one. For many, the illness can be tied directly to the extreme stress of their loss. In the case of great loss, grief and stress are usually prolonged and the occurrence of illness could occur even further down the road. Vigilant self-care during this period is vitally important.

Any chronic medical problems we may have can become worse following our loss because of stress and the potential for us to neglect our self-care. This may especially be a problem if we have been a caregiver for our lost loved one and were already stressed and exhausted when the loss occurred. Also, we may have been so focused on our loved one that we ignored any symptoms or health issues we might have had.

I strongly recommend that you plan to visit your health care provider for a checkup during the period when you are trying to get your life back together following your loss. If you don't have a regular health care provider, now is the time to find one. Plan regular wellness visits and do not ignore any symptoms or health issues that arise.

This is a time to take really good care of yourself and to not ignore any sign or symptom that you may notice but are unsure about. Have it checked out! Either it will bring you peace of mind or you may catch something early so it doesn't turn into a more serious problem.

> *Randy, a sixty-four-year-old financial consultant, had lost his wife of over thirty years during the past year. He came to see me for hypnotherapy for the sleep problems he had been having. He explained that he had been experiencing so much fatigue that he was having difficulty concentrating at work. He also described having a persistent cough and some hoarseness but believed that was because he had started smoking again after his wife's diagnosis. A recurring dream he had been having puzzled him and often woke him up when he did finally fall asleep. In the dream, it appeared that a woman was having a heart attack and paramedics were administering cardiopulmonary resuscitation (CPR). He explained that his wife had died of cancer, not heart problems.*

Randy had not been to see his physician since his wife had been diagnosed with breast cancer three years earlier, and he admitted that he had been under a lot of stress. I recommended that he go for a complete physical examination, so we could rule out any physical problems before proceeding with hypnotherapy sessions for his insomnia. We concentrated on relieving his stress instead. I also recommended that he take some quiet time to reflect on his recurring dream and see if he could gain any clarity about it.

Randy called me a week later to tell me he was having surgery to correct a thoracic aortic aneurysm. That is a bulging of the wall of the aorta, the major blood vessel that carries blood from your heart to your body. Often there are no symptoms of this condition, and should the wall burst, the results are typically catastrophic. Randy was convinced that his recurring dream was trying to warn him about his cardiovascular problem.

Our Higher Self is aware of any problems that may be occurring in our body and tries to let us know so we can do something about it. Thus, it is important to pay attention to any recurring dreams, persistent thoughts about our health, or uneasiness we may feel about our health. Connecting with our Higher Self will provide us with guidance regarding our health and urge us to take the action needed to alleviate the problem.

THE POTENTIAL FOR AN ACCIDENT

Another potential risk is that of a motor vehicle accident, a fall, or some other type of accident. The reason for this is that mourning can cause distraction. Grieving has the same effect on the brain as alcohol.

Philip, a forty-two-year-old salesman who sells large industrial equipment, came to one of my Great Loss workshops. He explained that he had been putting a tremendous amount of time and resources into selling the equipment to outfit a new plant that would be opening soon. It was the kind of sale that could make or break his company, and a lot of people were counting on him. It appeared that he had made the sale and only needed to obtain final signatures when a former coworker who had started his own company stole the sale at the very last minute. Philip was frustrated and angry and reported that he felt like a failure.

It had taken a lot of effort for Philip to attend the workshop, as he had a full cast on his left leg and had to navigate on crutches. The story that unfolded was that he had been pacing on the deck of his house ruminating on how he could have prevented what had happened when he absentmindedly walked right off the top step, breaking his leg in two places from the resulting fall. That was what had made him decide to attend the workshop.

There was another man at the workshop who had also experienced a sales failure, and the two of them became friends. They both realized, through discussion in the workshop, that they were suffering from depression, and decided that it was time to do something about it. They went on to attend a men's therapy group together, something that both said they probably would not have done without the support of the other.

Reliving memories of our loss can lead to distraction and a potential accident. Thus, it is important to be aware of this possibility while driving or at any other time that we might sustain an accident.

PERSISTENT SLEEP PROBLEMS

It is common for people to experience changes in their sleep patterns when grieving, but it's easy to overlook because there are so many other more obvious and painful stressors during this time. Mourners may have trouble falling asleep or staying asleep, or may even sleep too much. Anxiety about stressors that have occurred because of the loss, such as financial problems, intrusive thoughts, or sleeping in a bed that you used to share with your partner, can affect sleep. Long-term sleep deficits can have a negative impact not only on our emotional outlook, memory, and ability to think and concentrate but also on our bodies.

Not getting enough sleep can make us tired, cranky, and out of sorts the next day, but missing out on the recommended seven to nine hours of sleep over an extended period of time can cause other problems as well. The long-term effects of sleep deprivation are real and can put our physical health at risk. Sleep deprivation weakens our immunity and can cause poor balance and a lowered sex drive, make us more prone to weight gain, and put us at higher risk for elevated blood pressure, diabetes, heart disease, cancer, and stroke.

As if that were not bad enough, a lack of sleep can accelerate skin aging and decrease bone density. When we don't get enough sleep, we can feel overwhelmed more easily. A lack of sleep can also make us feel too tired to exercise and engage in important self-care.

Disrupted sleep patterns were a major problem for me in the first two and a half years following the loss of my daughter. I reverted to a sleep schedule that I had adopted when my ex-husband was a resident spending long hours at the hospital and my daughter was just a toddler. I was completing my PhD at the time and would spend my afternoons and evenings with her. I would start to do my academic work only after she had gone to sleep. I would then usually stay up until around 3:00 to 4:00 a.m., and because life kept on going, I would be up early the next morning.

I found that I was tired all the time after my daughter's death because I was following the same sleep schedule that I'd had back then, and I had great difficulty in trying to change it. I wondered later if my difficulty in moving out of this sleep pattern had to do with a subconscious attempt to recapture the closeness my daughter and I had shared during those early years.

It is common to have difficulty getting back to a healthy sleep schedule after great loss. Here are some tips for improving sleep. These are suggestions that I give to my patients and that I used myself when I was experiencing sleep difficulties in the aftermath of my great loss.

- Get at least ten minutes of natural light each day. This helps set our internal clock, which regulates sleep.
- Get at least thirty minutes of regular exercise each day in the morning or early afternoon. Avoid exercising too close to bedtime.
- Nap only in the early afternoon and for no longer than thirty minutes.
- Avoid alcohol during the last few hours before bedtime. Avoid caffeine after lunch and/or cut down your total caffeine intake.
- Make sure your bed is large enough to allow you to stretch and move freely. Also, make sure that your mattress is comfortable for you and that you have comfortable pillows and bedding. This is not a luxury, but is essential for good sleep.

- Your bedroom should be quiet, dark, and at a comfortable temperature, with adequate ventilation. If your environment is noisy, either wear earplugs or use a sound machine to mask the noise. Make sure your room is dark during sleeping hours. If necessary, block out streetlights or early morning sunlight. Use your bedroom for sleep and sex only.

- Keep a regular bedtime schedule, including on weekends.

- Avoid heavy, rich food within two hours of bedtime, although a light snack before bedtime can be helpful. Try a snack that includes the amino acid tryptophan, which can promote sleep. Adding calcium and some carbohydrates is even better. Some examples include a glass of milk with half a turkey or peanut butter sandwich, whole grain cereal with skim milk or yogurt, or a banana with a hot cup of chamomile tea. Foods that can keep you up are rich, fatty foods. Before bedtime, avoid drinking too much liquid or alcohol or consuming foods containing caffeine, such as chocolate.

- Develop a relaxing bedtime routine in which you quiet your mind and release worries. You might try listening to soft music or books on tape, meditating, and/or doing some light reading.

- If you awaken during the night and can't fall back to sleep, try to stay relaxed. You might try doing a relaxation exercise in which you systematically relax various parts of your body, meditate, visualize, or even count sheep. After fifteen minutes, get up and engage in a quiet activity, keeping the lights dim. You could try eating a light snack, but avoid teaching your body to expect a meal in the middle of the night.

PROLONGED DIFFICULTY WITH FATIGUE

The impact of a great loss is more intense than that of other losses we have experienced in our lives, and generally it will take longer for recovery. Thus, some of the physical effects experienced earlier in the grieving process may be prolonged. It may take some time before the fatigue resolves and we are again able to maintain a healthy daily routine.

The fatigue experienced in the early period following our loss can be persistent and turn into chronic exhaustion. A tiredness can set in that makes even routine tasks difficult. It feels like we are dragging ourselves from one thing to another, as there is little heart in what we do. As several of the participants in my Great Loss workshops have described it, we just feel dead inside.

After some time has passed since our loss, there is an unspoken expectation that it is time to get over it. Thus, we put on a mask and fake it. A few of the people around us may understand that we are still feeling the pain, but they do not know what to do with it. So we go through the motions, but our performance is not what it was. Grief is incredibly demanding, and fatigue is the natural result.

I experienced heavy fatigue for over two years after the loss of my daughter. While I did get back to my practice and to many of my social activities much sooner, it took tremendous effort. The act of getting up and getting dressed was a trial, and I had to guard against being late for appointments. I found myself wanting to back out of social engagements at the last minute, as I had no enthusiasm for anything.

I began to think my inability to bounce back had to do with my age, as I was getting older. I started thinking that I would never experience my usual high energy level again. However, I am happy to report that with intensive self-care and healing, as described in the following pages, my energy came bounding back.

Here is a list of tips that I give to my patients to combat fatigue and that were helpful to me as I struggled to get beyond the exhaustion:

- Rule out health problems. Fatigue is a common symptom of many illnesses. Even though fatigue is often experienced for an extended period after a great loss, it is important to make sure that an illness is not making the situation worse. Fatigue is also a common side effect of many medications, such as blood pressure medications, antihistamines, diuretics, and others.

- Increase your physical activity. Regular exercise boosts energy levels and improves the functioning of the heart, lungs, and muscles. Any exercise is good, but yoga may be especially effective for boosting energy.

- Drink plenty of water. Dehydration can contribute to fatigue as well as decrease alertness and our ability to concentrate. Urine should be pale yellow. If it is darker, drink more water.

- Go with the natural flow of your body's energy. Individual differences in daily energy patterns are determined by brain structure and genetics and are difficult to change. Instead, become aware of your own circadian rhythms and take advantage of your peak energy levels in planning your activities. While conventional wisdom may advise early to bed and early to rise, that may not be a good fit for you. If staying up late works better for you, then make sure you give yourself adequate time to get a good night's sleep before arising.

- Shed extra weight. Losing weight can provide a powerful boost in energy. A decrease in body fat improves mood, vigor, and quality of life.

- Eat more often. Eating smaller meals more frequently during the day can help to stabilize blood sugar levels and thus lessen fatigue. Favoring whole grains and complex carbohydrates, which take longer to digest than refined carbohydrates such as white flour and sugar, helps prevent blood sugar fluctuations.

- Take regular rest breaks during the day. Sit down, put your feet up, and relax for ten to twenty minutes.

A prolonged period of fatigue can turn into a condition called chronic fatigue syndrome, in which you feel so tired that you can hardly complete normal daily activities. This is unlikely, but if your fatigue persists and is not relieved by rest and sleep, you feel worse after physical activity, and you have trouble concentrating and multitasking, you may want to check with your health care provider.

The exact cause of chronic fatigue syndrome is unknown, and diagnosis is complicated because there is no single test to detect it and the symptoms can overlap with many other health problems. While there is no cure for this syndrome, symptomatic treatment is available. You may also benefit from seeking counseling to build adaptive skills and address depression, attending to sleep problems, and engaging in exercise that starts at a low intensity and gradually builds.

GETTING BACK TO HEALTHY EATING

Regardless of the type of loss experienced, appetite and food intake are usually affected, and with a great loss, these effects can be persistent. You might experience either an increased appetite or a loss of appetite. Food cravings and/or intolerances may also be a problem for a while.

Food can easily become a way in which we seek comfort. The death of a loved one or another major loss can make us feel as though nothing will ever feel good again, so the small pleasure of allowing ourselves to eat whatever we want can temporarily ease the pain. This gives us a dopamine high and temporarily distracts us. Of course, the relief does not last long, and overeating can have unwanted long-term consequences.

On the flip side, you may experience a prolonged loss of appetite and lack of interest in food. From a nutritional perspective, this can lead to undernutrition and weight loss. Attending to healthy eating as a part of our self-care during physical recovery from loss is essential to good health in the future.

Eating and managing daily life continued to be a problem for me for quite some time. Initially I went through a period of eating little and having strange food cravings and intolerances. I craved pink grapefruit juice and later crispy french fries. I could hardly tolerate meat, especially chicken. Fatigue and poor sleep meant my energy level was low and I lacked the motivation to shop and prepare nutritious meals. Also, my appetite was erratic for quite some time.

For the first year, if I was not having lunch with one of my friends or dinner with my romantic partner and only picking at the nutritious food on my plate, I wanted only candy and junk food. I gained over twenty pounds during that time. Here are some suggestions for maintaining nutrition and getting back to healthy eating:

- Keep it simple. Concentrate on easy-to-prepare or prepared foods and fresh fruits and vegetables. Another option may be to consider a meal service for the delivery of prepared meals or ingredients with instructions for meal preparation.
- Consider having a friend or family member shop for you, or have groceries delivered until you feel better able to handle things.
- Listen to your body and choose to eat the healthy foods that you desire or that you used to enjoy. Be sure to have easy, healthy snacks on hand.
- Plan to eat smaller meals more frequently if a regular meal schedule is not working for you. Do not go for prolonged periods without eating anything.
- Monitor your weight to make sure you are not either gaining or losing weight. We all have normal fluctuations in our weight, so look for trends over time.

Experiencing a prolonged period of fatigue, difficulty in getting enough sleep and rest, eating in a healthy manner, exercising, taking care of our bodies, and managing our household and daily routine can be a real challenge when we have been doing the work of grieving over a prolonged period of time. Grief takes an incredible amount of energy. I found that I was always behind in things, late to social activities, and dropping the ball on keeping everything together. It wasn't that I didn't know what to do; it was that I had difficulty getting it all done. My life felt very unbalanced for a while.

In reconnecting with life after loss, we must find a new normal that fits our changed circumstances. What helped me during that time was simplifying my activities, setting up a schedule that included time for relaxation and meditation, and getting outside support where I needed it. Gradually my concentration improved, my energy increased, and things begin to fall into place. It took a much longer time than I had anticipated and required some effort to get back into balance.

BROKEN HEART SYNDROME

With a great loss, we probably feel that we do experience a broken heart on the emotional level, but it can be a physical experience as well. Broken heart syndrome, or takotsubo cardiomyopathy, is a ballooning of the apex (lower part) of the left ventricle of the heart, which disrupts the heart's normal pumping action. This is a temporary heart condition that can be brought on by stressful situations such as great loss. People who experience this may have sudden chest pain or think they are having a heart attack. Most of the symptoms typically clear up in one to four weeks, and most people recover fully within two months. However, when these symptoms occur, it is important to have them evaluated immediately, as there is the possibility that a real heart attack might be occurring.

ASSISTANCE FROM OUR HIGHER SELF
AND THE SPIRITUAL REALM

During this time, our Higher Self is quietly speaking to us, trying to calm us and help us relax, but because of our distress, we are unlikely to be aware of these ministrations. If you have lost a loved one, be assured that your loved one is not really gone and is trying to reach out and comfort you. An example of when this is most likely happening is when we experience a normal part of grieving called a *grief burst*.

A grief burst is a moment when you are overcome by emotion thinking about the loss that you have experienced. These unpredictable times may be triggered by a memory, such as when you see, hear, or read something that reminds you of your lost loved one. It happened to me in the grocery store one day when I passed a section where I used to pick up some of my daughter's favorite foods. This can happen months or even years after the loss.

These episodes are usually short-lived and followed by a period of calm. After I was able to achieve afterlife communication with my daughter, I learned that she or my guides and angels are always there to comfort me when this happens. That is why these episodes are relatively short-lived and are always followed by a period of calmness.

I will discuss afterlife communication in chapter 9. If we take time to rest, reflect, and meditate, we may become more aware of the comfort and loving energy coming from our departed loved one and our spiritual helpers.

Ironically, given the likelihood of sleep problems after a great loss, another time when we may experience a connection with our departed loved one is in a dream. Initially grief can block our loved one from capturing our awareness. However, our Higher Self connects with our loved one regularly at night as we sleep. This is especially true during the first couple of years after they have made their transition back to the spirit world. After that, visits continue but may be less frequent, based on our need, according to information I have received during afterlife communication sessions.

My first awareness of a dream encounter occurred about three months after the death of my daughter. After tossing and turning for much of the night, I decided to get up but then fell into a deep sleep while sitting on the couch and had a dream.

I found myself standing a few feet in front of my daughter as she was sitting at her desk and working on her laptop. She looked radiant, glowing, and happy. We smiled at each other and I asked her what she was going to do today. She said, "Oh, I think I will go for a ride." I asked excitedly if I could go with her, but then I realized that this could not be because she was no longer living, even though it seemed so real. She gave me a Mona Lisa smile and replied, "No, it's not your time."

After I awakened, it still seemed so real. Then I realized that it was real and that I had been visited by her. Dream visitations are usually very vivid and leave no doubt in your mind that you have been in contact with your loved one. Once I realized that, it was as if a great burden had been lifted from my shoulders. Although I knew I still had a lot of healing to do, I knew that day that she was okay and that I was going to be okay too.

Great loss is likely to result in prolonged grieving and stress. This impacts all aspects of our being, physical as well as psychological and spiritual. This presents an opportunity for us to care for ourselves lovingly as we face our personal tragedy, with a chance to become stronger and more resilient as we do so. Psychological issues following great loss are addressed in the next chapter.

Here are some ways to address the physical consequences of great loss:

- Visit your health care provider for a checkup.
- Do not ignore any symptoms or health issues.
- Be aware of distraction and the potential for an accident.
- Get adequate rest and sleep.
- Maintain healthy nutrition and stay well hydrated.
- Pay attention to any dreams, thoughts, and feelings about your health.

EXERCISE

ASSESS YOUR PHYSICAL SELF-CARE

Assess your physical health and then take action to correct any deficits.

- Are you experiencing any troublesome signs or symptoms?
- When was your last physical examination? Is it time to schedule one?
- Are you getting an adequate amount of sleep and rest?
- How is your energy level?
- Are you getting any exercise?
- Are you eating in a healthy manner?
- What is your current health status?

CHAPTER SEVEN

COPING WITH THE PSYCHOLOGICAL AFTERMATH OF GREAT LOSS

A common element of great loss is that we feel as if our lives have been upended. Whether we are blindsided by our spouse seeking a divorce, lose our place of long-term employment, become disabled from a chronic illness or injury, or lose a loved one, our loss will force us to face several long-term psychological challenges. We have made it through the initial stages of grieving and now new realities are setting in.

Grief and loss can change almost every aspect of our daily routines. We might no longer have a spouse to depend upon and socialize with. If we have lost a job or career opportunity, we may no longer have any structure to our days or a place to go every day. A chronic illness may require us to substantially change our lifestyle. With a disability, we may have to retrain ourselves to handle even basic tasks of everyday living. It is difficult to fully accept loss. The challenge is to find new ways of living and being to replace those that we have lost.

Change forces us to pause and examine our lives to gain perspective. We are faced with many choices, shifts, and transitions throughout our lives. Each time we make a choice, we have a small loss of the other option. We also gain what we did choose. This system helps us move forward in our lives, but the process is disrupted when we experience a great loss. Our loss can leave us temporarily frozen and unable to make choices. Yet one of the wonderful things about human beings is that we are adaptable, even in the face of significant loss.

Our loss has left a void in our lives. I do not think that we recover from great loss, but rather we integrate the experience into who we are. We are now someone who has experienced tragedy. Emerging from our grief into a new life is more of an adaptation than a recovery. Great loss changes us and adds to our Soul wisdom. We must incorporate this change into our human character and personality as well.

Sometimes it can seem impossible to see any positive change amidst the tragic one that we have experienced, but change also opens new opportunities. Just like the seasons of the year, we keep on living and growing, and we can thrive again.

Think of our body, an exemplar of survival, continuing to do what it always does despite our despair and uncertainty. The amazing wisdom and resilience of our body is a testament to the continuation of our existence. The survival mechanism of the body informs the mind, and after we have passed through the early stages of grieving, we become aware of new challenges that await us as we adapt to our loss.

Initially we may be preoccupied with just getting through each day, but when the heavy early grief passes and our confusion clears, our needs shift from basic survival to a fuller vision of our life and what it might hold in the future. This is the time to reflect on who we really are and who we want to become. Just thinking about the future can make us feel anxious.

COPING WITH THE UNDERLYING ANXIETY

An important characteristic of the period after our heavy grief has passed and before we have reached a new equilibrium is a free-floating, underlying anxiety. Our great loss has knocked us out of our comfort zone and we have not yet found another safe harbor. I think we are largely unaware that we are experiencing this, but rather we just feel ill at ease. What the future may hold is unknown at this point, and we likely are feeling that it will be bleak given what we have lost.

Loss of a loved one upon whom we have been emotionally dependent through death, divorce, or a breakup may be behind this reaction. The occurrence of a death can give rise to fears of our own death. Loss of a job or loss of our main provider can create financial anxiety.

While this is an uncomfortable place to be, I urge you not to rush to move beyond this time. It is a period that is rife with potential for creating a better future. To make the most of this time, it is helpful to find ways to reduce this anxiety as we get to know ourselves better and tune in to our inner guidance.

Many of the suggestions in the previous chapter, such as exercising, meditating, eating a healthy diet, and getting adequate rest and sleep, can help reduce anxiety as well. While there are many ways to reduce our anxiety during this period, one that I used successfully and that I regularly recommend to my patients is the following simple relaxation technique.

EXERCISE

RELAXATION TECHNIQUE

This exercise has three parts. First, focus on your breath and begin by taking long, slow breaths. As you do so, just allow any distracting thoughts or sensations to drift away and keep focusing on your breath. When your distracting thoughts quiet, proceed to the next part.

Next, mentally scan your body to find any places or groups of muscles that feel tense and tight. Clench the area tightly, hold, then let go, allowing the tension to drain away. When you've released the physical tension, move to the last part of the exercise.

Lastly, bring to mind a special serene place, one that you find particularly relaxing. Imagine yourself there and enjoy taking a super effective mini vacation from the anxiety that you have been experiencing. Using this relaxation technique for even a few minutes can have a very beneficial effect. Doing it several times a day can markedly reduce the anxiety that is so characteristic of this period.

REFORMULATING OUR IDENTITY

Great loss impacts our sense of identity and leads us to examine how we define who we are. It makes us question the false identity that we had built up by focusing on someone or something outside of ourselves. The option of continuing in the same manner has been taken away from us by our loss. It feels like the person we once were is lost and the person facing us in the mirror is someone we do not really know.

This is a time when we can drop the mask that we typically wear to protect ourselves and see who is there underneath. Loss opens us up to a world of self-discovery and healing. The goal is to identify with our inner self. This will enable us to develop and nurture those choices that are consistent with our Soul self and the plans that we made for this lifetime.

Before my loss occurred, I had become strongly focused on helping my daughter recover from the violence she had experienced. As I became more involved in her life, my own interests became secondary. Even though I continued with my professional activities, the primary way that I was defining myself then was as a mother. With the loss of my only child, this role came to a screeching halt. I felt as if I had lost my primary identity.

Another way we might feel that we have lost our identity is when we have been defining ourselves by our couplehood but now have lost our spouse or significant other.

Daisy, one of my patients, lost her husband of forty years through an extended illness. They had met right after she graduated from high school and were married shortly thereafter. He had just established an insurance business, and she came to work with him in the office in a supportive role. They had no children, traveled, and spent a lot of their free time together. Her interests became whatever he was interested in, and she considered her marriage to be her life. When he became ill, they sold the business and she devoted herself to caring for him for the five years before his death. Having never developed any of her own interests, as a fifty-nine-year-old widow, she had no idea who she really was anymore.

What was most helpful to Daisy was journaling. She had always liked to get up very early in the morning, and she used this time to write down her feelings each day. I suggested that she reflect on what she had loved to do when she was single and to recall those things she had planned to do when she had time but had never gotten around to. The first thing she came up with was her love of reading, which she had not had time for in a very long while. The other thing that came up initially was that she had always planned to do some volunteer work with children when the time was right.

The local library proved to be a beginning solution for her. She went there to find some good books to read. When talking with one of librarians, she learned about children's story time and the need for volunteer readers. She promptly volunteered. She also ended up joining one of the women's book clubs offered. It is only a beginning, but she is on her way.

Other people identify primarily with their career role and do not see themselves as ever wanting to give up their work. Or their identity might be tied to a role in a religious or charitable organization.

Ralph is a fifty-two-year-old ophthalmologist who specializes in cataract and other eye surgeries. While he loves his work, it is his role on the board of his church that really gives meaning to his life. He has been involved with the community outreach activities of the church and has organized and directed several programs to assist low-income residents who live in an adjacent neighborhood. He has even cut back on his practice hours to spend more time on these projects.

Ralph's latest initiative became quite controversial among church members. Despite his best efforts to promote the program, the board voted to withdraw from the project. There were long, bitter discussions regarding this, and he became quite discouraged and alienated from the group. He ended up resigning from the board but was still attending the church. The loss of this important role, however, seriously affected his sense of identity. He developed a mild depression and was seriously considering leaving the church. His family could not understand what was going on, and this was very stressful for him.

Ralph came to see me initially for hypnotherapy for stress reduction and then went on to do a past life regression. Following suggestions made by his guides during this session, he started meditating and exploring what he wanted to do with his life. These practices helped him clarify what he wanted in his future. He had some long discussions with his wife, and with her encouragement eventually cut his practice down to part-time. Now both of them are working with a volunteer community organization assisting low-income families.

We all hold multiple roles in our lives, and that is sometimes how we and others define who we are. It is not always easy for others to know, however, which of our roles we consider to be primary, which one serves as our anchor. Great loss entails losing what we consider to be our anchor. Even those closest to us may not realize how seriously our sense of identity has been impacted by our loss.

The roles we hold, however, are just an aspect of us. They do not represent who we fundamentally are on the inside. Our Higher Self, a part of our Soul self that resides within us during our human experience, is who we really are on the inside. Getting to know our Higher Self gives us access to inner guidance that will lead us to our life purpose, values, goals, and beliefs.

As we adapt to our loss, we face the challenge of reexamining and redefining who we are and how we now see ourselves. This enables us to expand more fully into who we want to become beyond our loss. The key is to come into alignment with our Higher Self. Great loss is an invitation that beckons us to honor our inner self and follow the winding path laid out before us. We will discuss how to go about doing that in the next chapter.

READJUSTING OUR RELATIONSHIPS

The grieving process can have an immense impact on our relationships. That is true not only of the relationship we have with our spouse or romantic partner but all our relationships. Our grieving puts an incredible strain on our existing relationships, as who we are as a person is temporarily altered as we grapple with our loss and seek a way to move forward.

Our close friends and loved ones may have difficulty coping with how we are mourning and may seem to be temporarily moving away from us. They may be very used to considering us a pillar of strength, and seeing us in the vulnerable state we are in could be hard for them to deal with. That is especially true if they are also dealing with their own grief. To seek solace, we may need to turn to other family members and friends or make new connections with others facing loss through a grief group.

After a significant loss, our relationship with our romantic partner or spouse will either get stronger or be strained. Realistically, it is likely to be stronger at times and strained at others, but it will undoubtedly change. My partner and I had both of these experiences after the death of my daughter, and at times I was not sure that we would make it. I thought I needed to leave the relationship, but we decided to stick with it and see where it went. Now, several years later, the relationship has become much stronger.

What I learned through this experience was that both of us were grieving in our own way at the same time. While my partner was tremendously supportive initially, later he needed the space and support to grieve as well. Also, I learned that there is a fine balance to being taken care of while we are in crisis. It can feel good at first but later feel smothering. Additionally, the caretaker can come to feel underappreciated. For us, good communication was the key to rebalancing our roles in the relationship.

If we have lost a loved one, another strain that can be put on our relationships is that it can cause us to confront our own mortality. The awareness that we and our family, friends, and partner are also going to die arises in us. This realization hits us at our core. This could cause us to commit more fully to a relationship because we feel that life is too short to be without love and support. Or it could cause us to end a relationship that we believe is not working.

Family relationships can also be disrupted when there is a death in the family, and this can have a serious impact on how family members relate to one another. The death of a family member who played an important role in the family will create a gap, and adjustments will need to be made. When a parent or the surviving parent dies, family traditions and expectations inevitably change. It is important for family members to be open about their own feelings and respectful of one another's feelings.

Relationships with our friends are likely to be affected as well in the aftermath of great loss. Again, friendships may be strengthened when friends are there to support you, but you may find that other friends will not be fully present or helpful. Also, friends with whom you are not as close may come forward and be there for you. This is especially likely if they have experienced a significant loss and can identify with what you are going through. In addition, as you begin to integrate how the loss has impacted you into your life, you may find it difficult to maintain relationships with some friends.

Although we can expect our relationships to change following a significant loss, as we cope and with the passage of time, we can expect some normalcy to return. We can reestablish some lost connections by forgiving those who were not there for us as we dealt with our grief.

We can also form new connections that reflect the newly discovered realities of our situation.

ADJUSTING OUR BELIEF SYSTEM

Loss and grief can challenge the basic assumptions we hold about how the world works. We each have a unique set of beliefs and assumptions through which we view the world and our place in it. Great loss can cause us to question everything we thought we knew.

Significant loss changes our outlook, impacting how we think and how we view ourselves. Because it felt as though we had no control over our loss, we can experience a sense of powerlessness and consequently have trouble making the changes that would help us move on with our lives. We are flooded with questions and doubts.

Perhaps the biggest question of all is "why?" Our challenge is to find a way to make sense of what happened and then adjust our belief system accordingly. As we integrate great loss into our lives, we must find a way to ascribe meaning to it.

Before our loss, we were either focusing on someone or something outside of ourselves or living such a distracted or superficial life that we never went very deep. Our loss calls for us to confront our own spirituality through reflecting on our beliefs and values and getting to know who we really are on the inside. Getting to know our inner self requires a high level of introspection and self-awareness. Loss invites us to go on a journey of self-discovery. It is a lifelong journey, and great loss opens us up to this adventure.

Thus, now is an excellent time to turn inward and recover lost aspects of ourselves. By working to connect with our Higher Self and tune in to our inner guidance, we can find new meaning and purpose in our lives. While grief's journey never really ends, our feelings of loss will soften. Hope for the future will emerge and we can then make plans and move forward in our lives. We will discuss how to connect with our Higher Self and tune in to inner guidance in chapter 8.

CONFIDENCE AND SENSITIVITY

Grief can diminish our sense of self-esteem and confidence. I felt like a failure after the death of my daughter, as I had been putting so much effort into helping her recover. That feeling was compounded when I learned that she had died of a drug overdose and had been using street drugs in addition to her psychotropic prescriptions. As a nurse, I felt that I should have spotted that. I had been worried about her growing dependence on prescribed sedatives but had not suspected that she had gone beyond that point.

In addition to a loss of confidence, our self-esteem can suffer following a loss. Such was the case for Sally.

Sally, a thirty-two-year-old-woman who had just gone through a divorce, came to see me because she was experiencing serious anxiety. She reported feeling unattractive and feeling out of place, both in social situations and at work, since her marriage had fallen apart. She reported that her ex-husband had been her biggest fan, and now she felt that she could not do anything very well anymore. It had been almost a year since they had separated, and her family was pressuring her to "get over it" and get on with her life.

We live in a culture that expects us to "get over" our grief after a certain amount of time has passed, but we are all unique in our response to loss and there is no timetable for it. Our self-esteem and confidence can be impacted by experiencing pressure from our friends and family regarding not moving beyond our grief quickly enough. This just compounds the loss in confidence that we most likely already feel because of our loss.

I assured Sally that she should take as much time as she needed to heal from the loss of her marriage. We worked on reducing her anxiety and rebuilding her confidence. Hypnotherapy sessions were very helpful for her. She also started on the program I outline in the next chapter for connecting with her Higher Self and tuning in to her inner guidance.

There is no substitute for listening to our inner guidance and accepting the assistance of our spiritual helpers. Following the guidance of our Higher Self will always lead us to what is best for us. Our spirit guides can provide us with additional insights and help us in unseen ways. Discovering our life purpose and striving to achieve it brings joy and fulfillment to our lives.

Another change that you may notice is a heightened sensitivity to the fragility and uncertainty of love and life. After a significant loss, it is common to become more aware of people's feelings and to develop greater compassion for others. There is an awareness that life is not so certain, that we can never be sure what tomorrow will bring.

This feeling of uncertainty can produce anxiety, but remembering that we are Souls here on earth having a human experience can help put this into perspective. We have come to earth to have experiences and to learn from them. It is our conscious self that experiences this anxiety. Our Soul self, residing within us as our Higher Self, views human life as an opportunity to advance toward enlightenment and chose to come here for these circumstances. Our Higher Self is peaceful and reassuring.

Connecting with our Higher Self can provide comfort and confidence to our conscious self. Our loss has disrupted our usual routine, giving us a special opportunity to make this connection. This is the spiritual gift of great loss. I discuss how to connect with your Higher Self in the next chapter.

Here are some ways to address the psychological aftermath of great loss:

- Use regular relaxation to reduce the anxiety you feel, including the relaxation technique described in this chapter.
- Give yourself permission to take all the time you need to heal.
- Record your insights as you redefine yourself in your post-loss situation.
- Reflect on who you want to become and how to get there.

- Readjust your relationships to fit who you are now.
- Examine and update your beliefs and assumptions about life.
- Claim the spiritual gift of great loss by connecting with your Higher Self.

EXERCISE

REVIEW YOUR CURRENT RELATIONSHIPS

Contemplate the following questions and give some thought to any changes you may wish to make.

- Are there any adjustments needed in your current relationships to better fit your new life circumstances?
- Do some of your relationships no longer fit you?
- Do you need to form new relationships to better fit your new life circumstances?

EXERCISE

REFLECT ON YOUR FEELINGS ABOUT LIFE SINCE YOUR LOSS

Write about your current view of life and what that might mean for your future.

- Have your beliefs changed since you experienced your loss?
- How might your new beliefs affect your life?

CHAPTER EIGHT

THE SPIRITUAL OPPORTUNITIES OF GREAT LOSS

We are forever changed by a great loss. It is as if the loss knocks out a bridge on the road we have been traveling and we do not have the option of continuing to go in that direction anymore. We can choose to do one of the following:

- We can just sit down right where we are and essentially give up. This happens when we are so devastated by our loss that we feel our life is over. We no longer want to put any effort into our lives. We figure, with pain like we are now experiencing, it just is not worth it.

  Michelle, a thirty-nine-year-old woman, essentially gave up on life after her divorce. She grew up in a religious family. Her father was a minister in a conservative church, and divorce was frowned upon. She was married for almost twenty years and they had one son. Her marriage was happy for several years, but then she and her husband grew apart and eventually hardly got along at all. However, for her, divorce was out of the question. She was tremendously angry when her husband left her, and vowed she would never forgive him. She actively tried to turn her son against his father and complained to both his family and hers about how he had abandoned her. She was uninterested in dating and initially tried to guilt her husband into coming back, but he insisted on divorce. She was unable to get past this loss and refused to move forward in her life. Over time, she became very bitter and disagreeable, having essentially given up on life.

- We can follow someone else. This happens when we find a replacement for the person we have lost and live vicariously through their life. We forget about our own hopes and dreams again and do not take advantage of any opportunities of our own.

- We can pursue something we see off in the distance. This happens when we replace what we have lost with another role or quest and continue focusing on something outside of ourselves. We become so immersed in our new activity that we do not take the time to explore what is inside of us.

Dave was a born salesman. At forty-eight years of age, he had been successful in selling automobiles, starting with used cars, then new ones, and on to owning his own dealership. With an economic downturn, he lost a lot of money and was forced to sell his business. This plunged him into depression.

He suffered a heart attack a few weeks later and continued to battle anxiety. While he was completing a cardiac rehabilitation program, he came to see me for hypnotherapy for stress management. He completed rehabilitation and was successfully controlling his stress, but he missed what he called "the thrill of the sale." When a sales opportunity came along, he jumped at the chance and once again began putting in long, stressful days. Despite the pleas of his family and the advice of his cardiologist, he went right back to the way he had been living before the loss of his dealership.

- We can find our own path. We are guided in doing this by our Higher Self, our personal spirit guide, and other spiritual helpers from our true home in the spirit realm. This requires deep reflection and getting to know ourselves better than we ever have. A renewed opportunity to find our own path and become our true self is the gift hidden in a great loss.

As a Soul, we made careful plans for the life we are now living while we were still at home in the spirit world. We came here with purpose and with specific intentions for what we wanted to learn and experience. Of course, our conscious self is not aware of this, as we agreed to forget who we really are and what we hoped to gain by coming here to earth so that we could have a realistic experience.

Our conscious self is not alone in this venture, as our true self, the Soul, resides within us as our Higher Self. Our Higher Self speaks to us continuously, in a quiet voice, reassuring us and giving us guidance to make the most of our earth incarnation. Some of us have never been connected to this rich resource within, and others may have lost this connection through focusing on someone or something outside of ourselves along the way. Or we may have been living such a busy and/or distracted life that we lost this connection that we may have had earlier in our lives.

Great loss is a shock that gives us a chance to change the direction of our lives. It provides us with a new beginning so that we can become whole. We can achieve this through connecting with our Higher Self and tuning in to our inner guidance. In doing this, we can not only increase the joy and fulfillment in our lives but also make significant progress in meeting the goals that we set for this lifetime.

CONNECTING WITH OUR HIGHER SELF

Our Higher Self, or inner self, is who we really are on the inside. It is the part of us that is in complete alignment with the Divine, the Source, the Infinite. Getting to know this inner self will reveal our true purpose, visions, goals, beliefs, values, and motivations. This is not what society dictates or who others think we should be, but who we learn that we are for ourselves.

To come to know our true self, we must spend time in introspection and develop a high level of self-awareness. This does not happen overnight, but rather is a lifelong quest. Now is the time to begin this remarkable journey of discovery with renewed energy.

Many of us have never given much thought to who we are on the inside, and thus we identify ourselves by the various roles that we hold in our lives. For example, we may see ourselves as a spouse, parent, employee, friend, son/daughter, and so on. Some of us have spent our whole lives creating ourselves around these identities.

Thus, when we lose one of our most important identities through the death of a loved one, divorce, loss of a job, or other changes, we are lost. That is because we have little awareness of who we are on the inside. We are limited in the degree to which we can express our own vision, goals, and beliefs beyond what is expected in these identities.

Perhaps we had an awareness of our inner self at one time but became disconnected from it through an overidentification with one of the roles in our lives. This is what happened to me as I became overly involved in my role as a mother through helping my daughter recover from the violence that she had experienced. Despite my strong spiritual background and one-time stable connection with my inner guidance, I lost this awareness as I became immersed in my daughter's recovery. Bill became overly involved in his role as a son.

Bill, a thirty-four-year-old patient of mine, was remarkably close to his parents and was entrenched in his identity as a son. He spent a lot of time with his parents and did a lot of things for them, often forgoing

other social opportunities to spend more time with them. It was import-
ant to him that they approve of his choices regarding his career, roman-
tic involvements, and community activities. Thus, when his parents
were both killed in a car accident several years ago, he was devastated
and paralyzed about moving forward with his life.

It is admirable to be a kind and loving mother or son/daughter. We just need to know who we are on the inside and have a commitment to pursuing our own goals and dreams, and then we can still be devoted to these roles. By connecting with our inner guidance, we can be committed to pursuing our own goals at the same time or maybe even through our commitment to these roles.

We all have free will and can manifest the life on earth that we desire. If we are not connected to who we really are, however, then we are probably just living our life for others. Living up to the expectations of others and helping them meet their goals is not the same as pursuing what we really want. To live a life of our own creation consciously, we must first get to know our inner, true self.

I worked with Bill on getting to know who he was on the inside. Next I share suggestions for finding your true self that worked for him and other patients.

GETTING TO KNOW YOUR TRUE SELF

The following actions are ones that I suggest to my patients and that I took as well as I was reconnecting with my Higher Self and returning to my own life path following my great loss:

- Take time to listen to yourself. Give yourself the time, space, and quiet to hear your inner voice.
- Live in the present moment as much as you can.
- Keep a daily journal to write about your feelings, thoughts, and observations.
- Meditate or engage in contemplative prayer on a regular basis.
- Listen to some of your favorite inspiring music.

- Spend time in nature.
- Record and interpret your dreams.
- Try using oracle cards for inspiration.
- Express yourself through creative activities.
- Learn more about yourself from observing your interactions with others.
- Get to know your opinions.
- Try new things.
- Schedule a Life between Lives session.
- Sit in silence each night before bed.

TAKE TIME TO LISTEN TO YOURSELF

The first step in tuning in to our Higher Self is to create the time, space, and quiet in our daily routine so we can hear the soft whisper of our inner voice. This whisper comes from who we really are on the inside. It can be easily drowned out by the loud noise of the opinions of others and the clamor of everyday life. Thus, we need to slow down and take some time for quiet reflection to increase our awareness of this inner voice.

I suggest pausing to do this for brief periods at various times each day and also setting aside a longer period to concentrate on getting to know your inner, true self. If you are a morning person, it will probably be best to do this early in the day. If you function better in the evening, do it then. Choosing a special place to do this may also be helpful.

Make sure it is a quiet place where you won't be disturbed. Sit comfortably, with pen and notebook in hand, close your eyes, and direct your attention inward. Imagine a beautiful golden liquid light flowing down from an unseen source above. As this beautiful light surrounds you, feel yourself relaxing completely. Focus your awareness within and ask your Higher Self for guidance. Sit quietly and listen. Write down any messages or guidance that you receive.

PRACTICE BEING IN THE PRESENT MOMENT

It is important to spend time in the present moment rather than fearing what might happen in the future or worrying about what happened in the past. Focusing on our breathing and/or our body can help us be in the present moment. Paying attention to the sights, sounds, and smells around us can also help. It is important to note our current emotions as well.

We do not need to spend hours at this. We can incorporate times of present moment awareness into our day a few seconds or minutes at a time. We can check in with ourselves periodically about how we are feeling or what we are thinking.

WRITE ABOUT YOUR FEELINGS, THOUGHTS, AND OBSERVATIONS

Plan to write about your feelings, thoughts, and observations consistently, every day if possible. This helps us process our thoughts and feelings. Be sure to date the entries. You can write a lot or just a little, as there are no rules. Be sure to keep this writing secure, as it is private and just for you.

You can write about what you are thinking and feeling and what you need and want right now. Do it quickly, so that your inner critic is silenced. Do not spend time trying to get it just right. Be as honest about what you are thinking and feeling as you can, even if it feels embarrassing. When you are finished writing for the day, it is helpful go back and reread what you have written and then try to summarize where you are at on that day in a sentence or two. You might also include any actions you could take.

Go back and read previous entries periodically and reflect on them. Look for patterns in what you have written and also note any progress you have made. You want to look for clues about your hopes and dreams, as this is how you come to know your Higher Self.

MEDITATE OR ENGAGE IN CONTEMPLATIVE PRAYER

Meditation and contemplative prayer quiet our mind and body, enabling us to better hear the quiet voice of our Higher Self. This helps us tap into the well of wisdom, guidance, and inspiration within us that at other times we are too distracted to notice.

There are numerous types of meditation that can be practiced, many of which require little or no training. Many books, videos, apps, and other online resources are available to help you get started if this is something you might be interested in doing. What all types of meditation have in common is that they narrow our focus, shutting out the outside world, and they still the body. Meditation has many benefits. Not only is it helpful in reducing anxiety, but it also provides us with the quiet we need to hear our inner voice.

A simple form of meditation is to sit quietly and focus on your breath. Then just allow your thoughts to drift away. Listen for anything that may come up. Even five minutes may be helpful to you, and then you can work toward sessions of fifteen to twenty minutes. You may not experience much other than relaxation during this time, but the practice can unlock a freer flow of information from your inner self at other times during the day or later on.

Contemplative prayer differs from traditional prayer in that while we talk to God or our higher power during traditional prayer, in contemplative prayer we listen. Also called centering prayer, it consists of sitting in silence, feeling the presence of God, and listening. This practice can have profound effects and potentially allow us to experience unconditional love and acceptance. We may also gain insights into our situation.

Contemplative prayer is not supported by some, but I have experienced the profound effects of this practice and have heard similar reports from my patients who have tried it. I believe that this can be the same experience that can occur during a Life between Lives session, when a powerful, unconditionally loving presence appears, leaving both me and the patient transformed, inspired, and intensely grateful.

LISTEN TO REFLECTIVE MUSIC

Listening to music increases our self-awareness, as it can resonate with our inner self. It helps us think about who we are and who we want to be, and can connect us to our inner guidance. This can help us discover our purpose and find ways to offer our unique gifts to the world.

The right music for us has a transcendent quality that can connect us to something greater than ourselves. Music has an energy that helps us connect to our inner self and the oneness of the universe. Since we are all unique, different kinds of music may have this quality for each of us. Take the time to find the music that resonates with you as a Soul.

SPEND TIME IN NATURE

When we spend time in nature, we realign with the life force that permeates all of creation. Nature is peaceful, serene, and still. This brings us to a state of calm and centeredness. It feels good to be out in the natural world and makes us feel a part of something greater than ourselves. This helps us focus our attention inward. The peaceful serenity that we can experience in natural settings creates the quiet we need to hear our inner voice.

RECORD AND INTERPRET YOUR DREAMS

Messages from our Higher Self may come to us in various ways, and interpreting our dreams can help us connect with some of them. It is estimated that we remember only about 10 percent of our dreams, and some of us hardly ever remember our dreams. We can, however, set the intention to remember significant dreams. When we do remember one, it is important to write it down, as we tend to forget them very quickly.

Most dreams have multiple meanings. A first step in retrieving the messages from a dream is to reflect on it for a while before attempting to figure it out. Pay attention to how the dream made you feel and your first impressions of potential meanings. Then you may wish to look up the meanings of symbols or events that appeared in the dream either online or in a dream interpretation book.

USE ORACLE CARDS FOR INSPIRATION

An oracle deck is a set of cards that help us connect to our Higher Self and the Divine. They are widely available and easy and fun to use. Because of the high value placed on logical thinking in our society, some may view them as silly, but they have the potential to be helpful to us in understanding ourselves and our experiences better.

Find a deck that appeals to you. You can find them in bookstores or search on YouTube or the internet to find one. Most decks come with a booklet that provides instructions for how to use the cards and interpretations of what each card means. You ask a question and then pull a card or cards from the deck and read the meanings.

If you are new to using oracle cards, I suggest that you start by asking what your inner self wants you to know. You can then reflect on the information you receive and determine how it will be helpful to you. As you become more familiar with the cards, you can ask more specific questions to obtain guidance. Be on the lookout for information that resonates with you.

ENGAGE IN CREATIVE ACTIVITIES

Creativity allows us to express ourselves. Engaging in creative activities allows us to get in the flow, a state in which we are completely absorbed in something and lose all sense of time. This state of flow nourishes our Soul and leaves us feeling inspired, calm, peaceful, and purposeful. This is a relaxed state in which we can more easily connect with our inner self.

BECOME AWARE OF HOW YOU INTERACT WITH OTHERS

We can make a point of noticing what we say, how others respond to our words, and how we respond to what is said to us. We can become aware of the cause and effect within our interactions and how these interactions make us feel on the inside. This allows us to discover essential knowledge about ourselves. Also, this awareness helps us express our true self more fully.

DISCOVER YOUR OPINIONS

It is important to listen to ourselves to determine what our views are about things. We do not want to bounce our ideas off other people right away. Instead, we need the time and space away from others to cultivate our own opinion on matters. Allowing ourselves to figure out how we feel before letting someone else in on it gives us an opportunity to tap into our feelings. If we do not take the time to do this, it is so easy to be influenced by what others are thinking.

We are free to change our mind if others make valid points, as that is how we learn and broaden our perspective. However, if we do not figure out what we believe or think first, it will remain hidden from us. Making a habit of figuring out what we believe and think first and then entering into dialogue with others with an open mind allows us to honor our inner self and be open to growth.

TRY NEW THINGS

If we try new things and then listen to ourselves about whether we like them or not, it can help us discover who we are on the inside. Most of us tend to do the same old things in the same old way. This is our comfort zone. We may not always like the new things we try, but the important thing is that we make that decision ourselves through listening to our inner self.

SCHEDULE A LIFE BETWEEN LIVES SESSION

During a Life between Lives session, our conscious self can make direct contact with our Higher Self and we can learn many things about ourselves. We can ask questions and receive answers from our guides and wise spiritual beings as well as from our Higher Self. This session can provide us with valuable information about who we are as a Soul, our life purpose during this incarnation, and ways that we can strengthen the connection between our conscious self and our Higher Self. We also may be able to make a connection with a deceased loved one during the session.

As we begin making more decisions based on our feelings, others in our life may be disappointed or even upset. We cannot let that stop us from making new discoveries about who we truly are. Through listening to our inner voice, we can determine how we genuinely feel about things and then act accordingly. Through aligning our inner self and conscious self in this manner, we become more authentic and achieve greater happiness and fulfillment in our lives.

SOME WAYS I RECONNECTED WITH MY HIGHER SELF

I engaged in several of the practices in the previous section as I worked to restore my connection with my inner guidance, and they might help you as well. Here are some of the things I did.

The first thing I resumed was keeping a daily journal. This is a practice I had found to be extremely helpful earlier in my life, but I had stopped doing it. Taking it up again was very comforting and allowed me to write about my thoughts and feelings.

I usually wrote in my journal in the morning with a cup of coffee. I would get in the mood by rereading the last entry or two and then focus on what I was currently feeling and thinking. The journal became like a close friend with whom I could share my most intimate thoughts and feelings. Somehow, by writing all this down, I gained clarity about what was going on within me.

I started meditating again, too, on a regular basis. I had received training in Transcendental Meditation years earlier and had practiced it consistently throughout the years. However, once I became so involved in my daughter's recovery, I dropped the practice completely. Getting back to it was very comforting and helpful.

Spending time outside in nature was another thing that was helpful to me. I have a beautiful wooded backyard with various areas for relaxing quietly. I would begin by watching what was going on around me. I watched the flight of birds and listened to their songs. I breathed in the fragrance of blooming flowers and the aromas of the woods. As I remained very still, small animals would begin to appear, and I silently enjoyed watching their antics.

What I noticed is that as I took in the beauty of my surroundings, a sense of peace would come over me. I found myself breathing more deeply and allowing some of the tension I typically carried in my neck and shoulders to drain away. Then a feeling of belongingness would envelop me. I would feel, "I belong here, and I am a part of all this."

Recording and analyzing my dreams proved to be especially useful in understanding what was going on with me and accessing some of my deeper feelings. After I had the first dream in which my daughter visited me, described in chapter 6, I started recording and analyzing my dreams. I found that the memory of what I had dreamed faded very quickly, so I kept a notebook by my bed to record them immediately.

Two of my good friends are interested in dreams, and we started sharing our dreams and helping each other analyze them. I also started looking up my dream symbols in dream books and online and found a lot of truly relevant information.

Sometimes explanations did not fit or just seemed confusing. When that happened, I would ask to have another dream to help me under-stand, and inevitably another dream that helped me understand would come along. This did not usually happen right away, so I kept a dream journal so I could make connections and see trends in the messages I was receiving.

I also returned to the practice of drawing a daily oracle card. Some-times the information fit exactly with what I was thinking and feeling. Other days I wasn't sure how the information might apply, but it always made me think and often helped me gain a new perspective.

One of the best ways I found to connect to my emotions was to listen to some of my favorite soulful music. Not only would this soothe me, but it inevitably led me to new insights as well. As I listened to the music, a clarity about my present state would arise and I would feel a connection to who I was on the inside.

Creativity allowed me to express myself. One of my earliest efforts was to do an acrylic painting of my daughter on canvas that I labeled "Last Look." I hung it in a prominent place where I could look at it often, and it brought me tremendous peace. Later I added other creative activities and always learned something about myself and where I was at that time. It seemed to be yet another way to connect to my inner guidance.

Making art gives form to the images that arise in our mind's eye in our dreams and during meditation. This provides us with knowledge about ourselves and helps us identify and release painful memories. It can also help us identify patterns in our lives. Creating art is a way to make a connection with our Higher Self.

One of my favorite practices, and one of the most successful for me, is sitting in silence each night before I go to bed. I sit in my favorite overstuffed chair in my living room with all the lights turned off. My intent is to be present and listen carefully to my inner voice.

When I first started doing this, a lot of meaningless chatter filled my head, but I just let these thoughts go and focused on being present and listening. Gradually, a different, quieter voice began to emerge. At first, most of the messages were about me taking better care of myself, which was something I needed to do at that time. I started thinking I was just making up these messages, as they became very reassuring and comforting. But because I always felt better afterward, I kept going. After a while, messages started coming that surprised me, as they were not about things that I had already been thinking about. Sitting in silence before bed is now a practice I do each night and one that I believe helps me make an effective link to my Higher Self.

One of the most healing things I did was to schedule a Life between Lives session with a very experienced and skillful Michael Newton Institute colleague. I share my Life between Lives session with you in chapter 11, along with what I learned from my great loss. As you will see, I made a truly heartfelt connection with my deceased daughter during this session.

The precious gift contained within the experience of a great loss is the opportunity to make a significant connection with our Higher Self and become aware of our inner guidance This enables us to get back to what we came to earth to accomplish. A wonderful adventure awaits us as we witness the unfolding of our authentic self as we awaken to our inner voice speaking lovingly to us.

EXERCISE

HAVE A CONVERSATION WITH YOUR HIGHER SELF

It may take some time for you to hear the guidance that your Higher Self is always broadcasting to you, but you can talk to your Higher Self in the meantime. Try talking to your Higher Self as if you were having a conversation. Do this in a private place where you can speak freely. Talk about what is going on in your life and how you feel about it. Ask questions and request guidance. After you have spoken, spend some time sitting quietly and listening. Write about this experience in your notebook.

CHAPTER NINE
HEALING OUR WOUNDS

To successfully integrate the experience of great loss into who we are, we must heal our wounds. The wounds that remain in the aftermath of our loss will vary according to the nature of our loss and the point that we are at in our individual lives. I would like to offer my experience as a guide to help you identify and bring healing to yours.

Several years after the death of my daughter, many things in my life had returned to normal, and I know my family and most of my friends thought that I had successfully moved beyond that tragedy. I could pretend that was the case, too, when I was busy during the day. However, when I was alone late at night or at quiet times during the day, a well of sadness would become apparent—one that I was afraid I might drown in. I felt bereft and broken at those times.

What I learned was that I was not broken, but rather that I had been broken open by my loss. All my past losses, fears, disappointments, and sadness that had accumulated over the years would come spilling out during those quiet, alone times. Unhealed loss and sadness from the past accumulates, taking up tremendous energy. Once we have been broken open and it starts to seep out, it is virtually impossible to bottle it up inside again. This makes it impossible to return to successful living without addressing it. Without our great loss, we might never have had the opportunity to clear out all of this pain and heal in this lifetime.

While this occurrence may make us feel intensely uncomfortable and delay our ability to move on with our lives, it represents yet another opportunity for healing presented to us by our loss. Caring for ourselves lovingly as we address this accumulated pain clears the way for a brighter future.

ENGAGING IN MAXIMUM SELF-CARE

When we are broken open by our great loss, we are in a vulnerable state. This is good news, because that it is one of the best states for us to be in to make deep changes and to advance spiritually. Being vulnerable is also the doorway to self-love. This is a time for us to get in touch with who we really are on the inside and to love who we find there.

Since I felt in need of some tender loving care, the first thing I tried was setting up a program of maximum self-care. This included nutritious meals and snacks, extra rest and sleep, increased exercise, leisure activities, long, luxurious baths, massage, and spa treatments, availability of fragrant hand soaps and lotions, and setting aside a day for me to do whatever I desired once a week. Maximum self-care may mean something else for you, but the idea is to pamper ourselves as we are healing.

The period following a great loss is a special time and a chance for us to focus on ourselves. Accepting the reality of what our life is like after our loss is important. It may not be what we would have chosen, but it is important to acknowledge what it now is. This can make us happier in the present and help us achieve a better future. The Soul values experience and what we can learn from it. The Soul advances by successfully adapting to the various experiences we encounter in our lives. Acknowledging our current reality will help us choose our dreams wisely and then work to achieve them.

This is a time to get to know ourselves better, to connect with our Higher Self and our inner guidance, and to truly appreciate who we are. Self-acceptance is the ability to unconditionally value all parts of ourselves, the good parts as well as those that we think need improvement. One of our greatest struggles in life is to accept and love ourselves for who we are, even with our flaws. Part of my self-care during the time after my great loss was to get to know myself well, imperfections and all. Also, my intention was to extend as much compassion and love to myself as I could.

Here are some self-care techniques and practices that worked for me. I went back to the practice of mindfulness, the art of being present in the moment, as often as I could. Years earlier, when I had done a visiting professorship in Thailand, I was able to learn about the practice of mindfulness from those who did it very well. Apart from my professional responsibilities, I had plenty of time during the period after my loss to develop this art.

Most of us probably think of mindfulness as meditation, and it is that, but it's also something more. It is living in a mindful way, aware of the present moment. The primary goal of mindfulness is to identify and reduce physical and emotional pain through the development of detached observation and awareness of what is going on in our consciousness. Mindfulness has the potential to transform the way we respond to life events because it enables us to be more aware of what we are thinking and feeling. There are many excellent books and videos available to help you learn more about mindfulness if you are interested. I have listed some in the recommended resources section at the end of the book.

Another thing I did was to go back over my life history, from the earliest times I could remember to the present. This exercise helped me identify incidents in my past that were still hurting. Uncovering these past hurts felt like I was lancing wounds that had healed over but were still festering inside. There was more to healing these past hurts than just identifying them, though, and the grief recovery group I joined helped me find a way to do that.

I found that I needed to go back and complete any relationship that was still causing me some emotional discomfort. To do this, I needed to be honest about what had really happened that was causing me pain and what my role in the situation was. I was able to complete the interaction by constructing what I wish I would have said or done to complete the interaction that had hurt me in a positive manner. Another thing I did during this period was keep a gratitude journal. I had heard about this many times in the past and thought it was a good idea but had just never gotten around to doing it. At first I found it almost impossible to do. I learned that I felt very ungrateful, having lost something so precious to me as my beloved daughter. To be honest, it took a great deal of effort for me to feel any genuine gratitude at that time.

What helped me make a breakthrough was one of my weekly grocery shopping trips. I always felt sad at these times, as a big part of my previous shopping had been selecting things that I thought my daughter would enjoy. On this day, it was the kindness of a fellow shopper that did it. She gave me a very warm smile and gently touched my arm as she passed me. It was as if a dam had burst, and I stood there in the aisle and wept openly, in my own little bubble.

When I regained my composure, I hastened around the corner to find the lady and thank her. She was nowhere to be found. I wonder still if I was touched by an angel that day, or at least a person doing the work of the angels. The kindness she showed me was something that I could genuinely feel grateful for. This encounter helped me recall all the kindnesses my friends and family had been showing me since my loss. From then on, I realized that I had a lot to be grateful for and vowed to pay it forward by being kind to others.

FACING RESIDUAL GRIEF HEAD-ON

After my loss, I also made the decision to avoid distraction and busyness and meet my accumulation of unresolved grief head-on. This was not easy for me, as keeping busy and distracted had been a way for me to avoid painful feelings. Here are some things that helped me break the busyness habit:

- I planned extra time in the morning to ease into the day. I went to bed a little earlier and got up earlier so I could have some extra time in the morning before starting my day. Being slower in the morning set the tone for the day, and I began to really enjoy this relaxed time.

- I scheduled "me time" and kept the commitment. I put time on my calendar for me to relax, reflect, or just do nothing. At first, I kept trying to fit other things in at those times, but I kept reminding myself that I needed this time.

- I limited my time on the computer. It was so easy for me to spend hours checking emails, surfing the web, and checking in with social media. I set some time limits and tried to stick to them. That was a difficult thing to do, but I could see that it was helping me slow down.

- I took relaxation breaks during the day. I started taking just a few minutes several times a day to breathe deeply and just be calm. I began to really enjoy these times.

I also set aside time for those feelings that I had been trying to avoid to arise. I wrote down everything I was feeling and what was attached to these feelings. I was a bit shocked that my relationship with my mother and the events of my earlier divorce kept coming up, as I thought that I had dealt with those feelings already. It became obvious to me that I could use some assistance in coping with these unresolved feelings, so I made an appointment with a counselor.

I saw the counselor twice before she suggested that I join a grief recovery group that she would be co-leading. I eagerly signed up for the group, which met once a week for eight weeks. I was blessed to have eleven other women and men of various ages and grief experiences with whom to share this remarkable experience. The program developed by John James and Russell Friedman is outlined in their book

The Grief Recovery Handbook. I highly recommend this book and a group led by one of their trained facilitators if you can find one in your area.

The content of this program, the skill of the two group facilitators, and the openness of my fellow group members were all very healing and reassuring. I started to feel better after the first couple of sessions, and by the end of the program I had a whole new perspective on my unresolved feelings. I went into the program thinking I would be able to deal with any unresolved feelings I had about the loss of my daughter, but I quickly realized that I had to go back further than that.

A particularly helpful feature of this grief recovery program is to identify any losses from our past that are still emotionally and spiritually incomplete. Through the task of reviewing my life history using their format, I was able to identify the losses I had experienced that were still carrying an emotional charge. Thus, during the eight-week program, I focused on my relationship with my mother.

I was surprised to discover how unbalanced my memories of that relationship were and was able to quickly identify my unresolved feelings about the relationship. It turned out that I was mainly recalling all the times when she had hurt me or not been there for me. I did not seem to remember much about all the special times we had spent together or the love and care she had shown me when I needed her the most. I also gained an appreciation of how difficult her life had been.

It appeared that I had conveniently forgotten about times when I had been difficult and times when I could have been there for my mother and was not. I felt ashamed and needed to forgive myself for this. I also needed to shed the feelings of victimhood that I had nurtured for years about poor little me and my difficult childhood. There were some things I needed to forgive my mother for as well. When I completed this passage, I was flooded with feelings of relief and genuine love and appreciation for my mother.

While this exercise was very healing, I was not finished. The next step for me was going back and doing the same thing regarding my relationship with my ex-husband and my relationship with my daughter.

I found it interesting that my memories of my ex-husband were predominantly negative, while my memories of my daughter were almost entirely positive. James and Russell suggest that this one-sided, distorted memory is really a function of a broken heart that does not know a better way to communicate the truth.[7]

By doing this work, I was able to see each relationship more realistically, appreciating the positive aspects as well as the negative ones. I was also able to complete unfinished business from each relationship and then genuinely appreciate what I had gained and learned from each experience. Completing a lost relationship does not mean forgetting, but rather bringing the loss to a comfortable resolution and harvesting the lessons from the experience. I will say more about reaping the lessons contained in loss in the next chapter.

THE HEALING BALM OF FORGIVENESS

I have learned that forgiveness is a vital part of healing old wounds from the past. As Souls in the spiritual realm, we are unconditionally forgiving. It is only our conscious self that needs to forgive in order to heal.

As I went through past relationships and events, it was relatively easy to identify the ones for which forgiveness was needed, because they were the ones that still held an emotional charge for me. Even after many years, I could still feel the hurt and anger as I recalled them. It took me much longer to realize that I had some things to apologize for as well, and even longer to realize that I needed to forgive myself too. The process of forgiveness holds within it the potential to learn so much about ourselves and to build Soul character.

Forgiving those who have wronged us is healing, as the person we hurt the most by holding on to resentment and anger is ourselves. Forgiveness is not about condoning what the other person did, giving in, or

7. John W. James and Russell Friedman, *The Grief Recovery Handbook* (New York: William Morrow, 2009), 118.

pretending that it really didn't matter. We should not force ourselves to get along with someone whom we fear may hurt us again.

If we are not quite ready to forgive completely, at least we can accept that the situation did happen and stop obsessing about the injury. It can be hard to get these thoughts out of our mind, but we can do so by challenging our negative thoughts and dealing with the stress that we are feeling. Suggestions from previous chapters on meditation, relaxation, and self-care can be helpful. This will allow us to let go of the emotional pain while still being true to ourselves.

Acceptance involves honoring all our feelings. The process also allows us to look more deeply into the situation and learn from it. From this perspective, we can examine our own contribution to the situation and view the offender's behavior with an understanding of their own personal struggles. While it is important for us to take the necessary steps to protect ourselves from further abuse, learning as much from the situation as we can helps us avoid repeating it.

We might ask ourselves if we have been in a similar situation previously with different people. Have we ever done the same thing to another or to ourselves? Is this situation similar to the way things have happened in our families?

In past life regressions, I have been impressed by how people who have been rejected, ridiculed, deceived, or abused in life will often let it all go with love once they reenter the spirit world. Instead of harboring any anger or resentment, they frequently focus on what they have learned from the experience and even feel gratitude for the lesson. I'm not suggesting that we attempt to go that far at this point, but rather that we forgive so that we can let go of the pain attached to the experience.

Advice received during Life between Lives sessions repeatedly stresses that forgiveness is about choosing peace and happiness over righteous anger. Energy consumed by holding on to grudges and nursing old wounds can be better utilized in pursuing our life purpose and creating a life of joy and fulfillment. It has been said that a life well lived is the best revenge.

If we have wronged another, it can be tremendously healing to make amends. We may not be able to do this directly if they have died or if we are estranged from them. However, we can communicate at the Soul level by sending them thoughts of apology and love.

Perhaps one of the hardest things is forgiving ourselves for what we feel we did or didn't do properly concerning our loss or past events. We may feel guilty, whether we have valid reasons to do so or not.

If, upon reflection, we find that there is some basis for our guilty feelings, then we can treat ourselves with compassion as we resolve the situation. First, we can accept responsibility for what happened and use the resulting remorse to change our behavior in a positive way. An apology or other action may be called for to reestablish trust.

The guilt may not be valid, however, and we may be unfairly blaming ourselves because we hold unrealistic expectations. People tend to view events as more predictable than they really are, which is called *hindsight bias*. This is particularly true when we feel that we should have been able to predict and therefore avoid a negative outcome. Unless we are able to let go of these feelings, we cannot turn our attention to our own future, because we will be stuck in the past.

We cannot change the past, but we can accept it and forgive ourselves. Here are some questions to ask ourselves: Can anything be done to change what happened? Why am I holding on to this? How can I use this opportunity to grow? If we have lost a loved one, recognizing signs that they are trying to let us know that they are still with us and still care can help us move on with our lives.

SIGNS FROM OUR DEPARTED LOVED ONES

The heaviness of my grieving made me unsure at first about signs that my daughter was near and trying to comfort me. I was still hospitalized following my knee surgery and had just been transferred to a rehabilitation unit. Late at night, when everyone had gone home and the unit was quiet, I became aware of the first sensations.

We are all connected on an energetic Soul level. The only difference is that our loved one is no longer in a physical body. On one of those early nights as I lay awake thinking about my daughter, I felt a sudden warmth accompanied by a sense of well-being. It also seemed as if someone had touched me lightly on the shoulder. This created a slight tingling sensation on my skin. Some people see an image of their departed loved one during these times.

You might not actually feel any sensations, but just have a sense that the person is close by. Trust your feelings. In past life regressions, I have heard so many times that shortly after their death, departed loved ones try to comfort the loved ones they have left behind. They also report staying near to their loved ones in the early period after their passing. If you sense the presence of your departed loved one, they most likely are there.

The other early sign I became aware of was smelling cigarette smoke when no one nearby was smoking. My daughter had continued to smoke even though I had been strongly encouraging her to quit for health reasons. Others report more pleasant aromas, such as their loved one's favorite perfume or the fragrance of their favorite flower. There are many other signs you might notice that a departed loved one is near. You might notice feathers or coins that appear unexpectedly in your path. After one of my very dear friends died of pancreatic cancer, many of her close friends reported seeing white feathers. I never did see any feathers, but one day when I was in my office seeing patients, my phone chirped, and it appeared that I had received a text message from her. She had also practiced as a healer, and that was one of the ways that we had really connected. The same thing happened on two other occasions. Her name appeared, but there was no actual message, other than perhaps the unspoken "I am here with you."

During the first several months following the loss of my daughter, as I was preparing for bed and turning off the lights, suddenly the television would come on and/or a light would switch back on. Another one of my dear friends lost her long-term partner after an extended illness as I was completing this book. She shared with me that on the night after his death, her porch lights blinked on and off again twice.

Because our deceased loved one is now pure energy, they can manipulate energy in any form. When you notice these occurrences, this is an indication of their presence. They are letting us know that they are still with us.

Later, toward the end of my first year of grieving, I decided to go to a spiritual conference that I had been scheduled to attend. While I was there, I did a filmed interview in an atrium with floor-to-ceiling windows on the third floor of the building, while sitting right next to the windows. In the middle of the interview, a bird came and perched on the outside of the window at my eye level and appeared to be looking right at me. It just continued to stay right there, attracting the notice of all who were in the room. I knew deep inside that this was a message from my daughter.

I have this encounter on film to remember it by, and I treasure it. Birds, butterflies, dragonflies, and even small animals can be a sign from our deceased loved ones. Typically, the messenger of this type appears in an unusual place, gets unusually close to you, and/or stays for an unusual amount of time. During a regression session, one patient reported sending a butterfly to comfort his wife after his death, as she had loved butterflies. He also reported that the bird, insect, or animal is very honored to carry this message of love and comfort for them.

HOW MEDIUMS CAN HELP

A spiritual medium is a person who can receive information from the spirit world and bring us messages from our deceased loved ones. They may be naturally gifted with the ability to do this, or perhaps they have attended a training program for those who are drawn to this endeavor. Mediums can bridge the gap between the living and those who have died.

Unfortunately, like me, you may not have been able to say goodbye to your loved one before they died. A medium can give us an opportunity to hear from our departed family member or friend one more time. This can be very comforting.

Before losing my daughter, I had already held a strong belief that our loved ones do not die, but continue to exist in another dimension. I understood that she had completed what she had come here to do or she had decided that it was not going to happen in this lifetime and had gone back home to the spirit world. I also knew that our love would endure and that I would be able to communicate with her again. What I did not understand was how the heaviness of my grief would block me from doing so initially.

I was having contact with my daughter in dreams, and there were those experiences that let me know she was still around and trying to comfort me and assure me that we were still connected. However, during that early period, I yearned for more direct communication and I had many questions. Luckily, I have several friends who are mediums, and they came to my rescue. They conveyed to me that she was doing fine and did not want me to be sad. They let me know that she was often right by my side during those early days.

An analysis of messages received by spiritual mediums reveals that there is a consistency in the information that is conveyed from our deceased loved ones. First, they want us to know that they are still here. While they are not participating in our day-to-day lives as they once did, they are still very much around. Often, the medium can provide evidence that our deceased loved ones are still aware of what is happening in our lives.

Second, our deceased loved ones want us to know that they are okay. They are experiencing the joy of being back home again, and any suffering they were experiencing as they left the earth is now behind them. When I learned that my daughter had died from a drug overdose, I worried about what her last minutes on earth had been like. A medium was able to reassure me that she did not even remember the incident.

I was also curious about how soon after her physical death she had crossed over to the other side. We have learned through Life between Lives sessions that sometimes Souls leave immediately after the death of their physical body, while others remain for a few days up to a week or two to comfort those they are leaving behind and bring a close to their earth experience. Often they attend their funeral or memorial service. Still others may remain for longer periods of time, not yet ready to leave the earth.

A medium was able to tell me that my daughter had crossed immediately to the other side, accompanied by my grandmother, who had died before she was born. I learned that my grandmother was staying with her and helping her get readjusted to her new state. This was very reassuring news for me to hear.

Another message frequently conveyed through a medium is "don't feel guilty." When someone dies by suicide or when a child dies, those left behind can feel weighed down by guilt. Hearing this comforting message can lift the guilt and allow survivors to move on.

About a month before the unexpected death of my daughter, I attended a program in which a medium spoke about her practice and did random readings for those assembled. I was surprised when my grandmother came through and her message for me had to do with my daughter. She told me, "You didn't do anything wrong and everything is okay." Of course, at the time, I thought she was forecasting a full recovery for my daughter and telling me that all my worrying about whether I was doing enough was needless. In retrospect, I think the events to come were already set into motion and she was trying to prevent me from feeling guilty afterward.

One other consistent message coming from our departed loved ones is "please be happy." They are now back home in the spirit world, reunited with their Soul family and friends and those who departed from this life before them. It is a joyous time, and they are surrounded by the peace, love, and acceptance of the spirit world. In this peaceful and harmonious state, they want us to be happy and make the most of the rest of our earth life. In my experience, if you have lost a spouse, they always encourage you to find love and be as happy as they are.

Of course, we do not need a medium to be able to communicate with our departed loved ones. We can always talk to them, either out loud or in our head. Rest assured that they can hear us, and we can develop our ability to hear what they are communicating to us as well.

ESTABLISHING AFTERLIFE COMMUNICATION

Yes, it is possible to communicate meaningfully with our departed loved ones. I mean more than just talking to them, but rather having a real conversation with them. There are many books, videos, and programs that tell stories of individuals who have been able to do just that, and they are very inspiring. However, the real proof comes when we can achieve this for ourselves. Nothing in my journey to move beyond my great loss was as healing as my first real conversation with my deceased daughter.

Today we are fortunate to have a variety of programs available to help us establish communication with our departed loved ones. One of the most exciting developments is the progress that has been made in establishing communication with Souls in the spirit realm through electronics. Two examples that you may wish to explore are electronic voice phenomena (EVP) and the SoulPhone Project.

EVP is a technique that uses electronics to make messages from those in the spirit world audible. According to Reverend Sheri Perl Migdol, when we play and record sound, our departed loved ones can use thought to change the sounds we provide into words that we can hear and understand. We retrieve these messages by playing back the recordings we have made. Directions for trying this technique can be found at www.sheriperl.com/evpguide.

The SoulPhone is a group of devices being developed at the University of Arizona for communicating with the deceased. According to Dr. Mark Pitstick, director of the SoulPhone Foundation, the devices being created are intended to allow us to have conversations with our loved ones who are now in the spiritual realm.[8] Research on this technology is being carried out by Dr. Gary Schwartz and his team at the Laboratory for Advances in Consciousness and Health at the University of Arizona.

However, I began at a simpler level. I would like to share the program I used and the wonderful results that it produced. I wanted to find a method that I could learn and use on my own. I started with the book *Afterlife Communication* by R. Craig Hogan, PhD.[9] Then, after examining several possibilities, I decided to try Dr. Hogan's free online program called "Self-Guided Afterlife Connections."[10] This self-guided program provides training and uses recorded hypnotic procedures to enable you to develop your own afterlife connection. You keep a journal while engaging in the program and receive feedback answering any questions you might have and providing additional suggestions.

Early in the program, I decided that the perfect place to be when my daughter and I had our conversations was on the covered patio outside her old room. That was where we would often sit and chat after she came home to live with me again after the assault. I planned to listen to the hypnotic recording there and hoped that I could make a connection.

One day I headed out that door intending to go into the backyard, not thinking of the program at all. As I started to cross the patio, a stream of information started filling my head. I stopped abruptly when I heard "Hoo-Do Guru," the name that my daughter had often used jokingly to refer to me in my spiritual explorations. I sank into my favorite patio chair and asked out loud, "Honey, is that you?"

I immediately got back the response, "Well, who do you think it is? Who else would it be?" And so began our first actual conversation.

---

8. Dr. Mark Pitstick, SoulPhone Foundation, "SoulPhone Device Overview," https://www.thesoulphonefoundation.org/soulphone-overview, and "SoulPhone Project Updates," https://www.thesoulphonefoundation.org/soulphone-update, accessed August 7, 2021.

9. R. Craig Hogan et al., *Afterlife Communication* (Loxahatchee, FL: Academy for Spiritual and Consciousness Studies Publications, 2014), 21–44.

10. R. Craig Hogan, "Self-Guided Afterlife Connections," Afterlife Research and Education Institute, accessed August 7, 2021, http://selfguided.spiritualunderstanding.org.

I did not hear what she was saying as an actual voice, but rather as a silent conversation in my head. The information was qualitatively different from my own thoughts and was delivered in the sassy, loving style that was very characteristic of my daughter. From then on, I no longer needed the hypnotic procedure to make a direct connection, but could do it on my own. The more often I made a connection to my daughter, the easier it became and the deeper our conversations became. I think that at first I might have thought I was just making it up, but hearing "Hoo-Do Guru" in such an unexpected way made a believer out of me.

The other thing I want to add here is that we have learned from Life between Lives sessions that our departed loved ones watch over us and send us love and encouragement. Once I was having one of those bad days when everything seemed to go wrong. The worst thing was that a project that was important to me was just not going anywhere. I was depressed and discouraged when I got home later that evening and just collapsed on the couch. Almost immediately I felt the familiar warmth and began hearing words of comfort and encouragement from my daughter. Our departed loved ones are there to comfort us when we need them, even though we may not always be aware of their ministrations.

EXERCISE

ESTABLISHING COMMUNICATION WITH A DEPARTED LOVED ONE

I have worked with many people who were open and interested in establishing communication with a departed loved one but were unsure about their ability to use the program I used or others like it. Therefore, I developed some suggestions to help them get started. This was all some of them needed, while others went on to use one of the programs for establishing afterlife communication listed in the recommended reading section. A few were satisfied with being able to feel the presence of their loved one and did not try to have actual conversations. Here are some suggestions to try:

- Learn more about who we really are, the spirit world, and how we are always connected. I suggest reading the first two books by Dr. Michael Newton, *Journey of Souls* and *Destiny of Souls,* to gain an understanding that (a) we don't die, but return home to the spirit world, (b) communication between those who have returned to the spirit world and those of us living on earth is possible, and (c) our loved ones who have returned to the spirit world reach out to comfort us and let us know they are still with us.

- Be open to the possibility that we can communicate with our departed loved ones. You may not fully believe in afterlife communication until you have actually experienced it. However, it is imperative that you be open to the possibility.

- Set aside some time and choose a quiet, private place for a meeting with your departed loved one. Mentally tell them that you will be there and want to visit with them during that time. This might be a place where you spent time together or a setting that had meaning to them.

- Bring a picture of your departed loved one to this meeting. I had an enlargement made of one of my favorite headshots of my daughter, which I focus on when I want to talk with her.

- Begin by greeting your departed loved one and talking to them as if they were present. You might tell them about what is going on in your life or talk about subjects that you know they were interested in when alive. Then sit in silent awareness, listening, sensing, and feeling. Attempt to detect their presence in any way that feels right to you.

- You may wish to record your experiences in your journal.

Once you have been able to feel the presence of your departed loved one or hear some initial words of response from them, consider trying one of the published programs designed to help you establish afterlife communication. A list of references is included in the recommended resources section at the end of the book.

———

The next thing I attempted was to uncover any lessons that were hidden within my great loss. I found that I was not able to clearly see the lessons of my loss until I had achieved a significant amount of healing. We will discuss this topic next.

Here are some suggestions to try to establish communication with a departed loved one:

- Engage in maximum self-care.
- Schedule time with a grief counselor.
- Join a grief recovery group.
- Forgive others and yourself as needed.
- Look for signs from departed loved ones.
- Have a reading with a medium.
- Establish afterlife communication with your lost loved one.

EXERCISE

DEVELOP A PLAN FOR MAXIMUM SELF-CARE

Self-care is not selfish, but rather is an important part of healing from a great loss. Consider making it a priority. The idea is to treat yourself lovingly. Start with small, manageable items. Think about your individual needs. We are all different, and your plan should fit you. It may be helpful to think about dividing your self-care into physical, psychological, spiritual, social, and occupational actions. Splurge in moderation by treating yourself to something you really want, provided it is financially feasible. Consider making your environment cozier or more pleasing to you. Be flexible and enjoy focusing on you and your needs.

CHAPTER TEN

HARVESTING THE LESSONS OF GREAT LOSS

Great loss, as it is defined in this book, is a monumental wake-up call. It is a reminder from our Higher Self to live an authentic, meaningful life. Experiencing great loss awakens us to the life we have been living. We may have been so invested in someone or something outside of ourselves that we have not been attending to our own life. Or, when things are going relatively smoothly, it is easy to fall into a kind of trance in which we forgo growth and true happiness for comfort and mild contentment.

Great loss forces us to examine how fulfilling our lives are. It presses us to remember the dreams we have yet to pursue, the adventures we have not yet taken, and the connections with others we have yet to make. If we have lost a loved one, we feel the fleeting, transient nature of life more acutely. These are the promptings from our Higher Self, reminding us that we are still here and that we still have more of our precious life on earth to lead.

ASSESSING OUR LIFE
BEFORE OUR GREAT LOSS

While following our inner guidance will lead us back to the plans we made for our current lifetime, assessing where we were before our loss can also help us move back into alignment with these plans. We can explore how we were living before our loss and the impact it had both on ourselves and on those around us.

EXERCISE

SELF-ASSESSMENT FOR INNER GUIDANCE
AND DISCOVERING YOUR LIFE PURPOSE

Here are some questions to help you assess your life before your loss occurred:

- Were you living the life you really wanted, or could life have been better for you and your loved ones?
- How fulfilling was your life? Were you pursuing your hopes and dreams, or were you focused on someone or something outside of yourself?
- Were you too busy and distracted to attend to how you were feeling inside?
- Was life comfortable but not truly satisfying?

Asking ourselves these questions and giving honest answers can help us connect to our inner guidance and discover our life purpose and the lessons we intended to learn during this incarnation.

When I did this assessment, I realized how busy and distracted I had been before the death of my daughter. I had no time to listen to or care for myself, as I had been so focused on her recovery. I was neglecting my romantic partner, my extended family, and my friends, but most of all, I was neglecting myself.

I realized that I needed to regain health, balance, and stability in my life so that I would be in a better position to create a life that was more in tune with my Higher Self and thus more fulfilling. What I think is helpful to improve our well-being is to envision the quality of life that we would like to have and then look at what is getting in the way. Even making small changes can help us move forward.

I also think that making our environment more pleasant can really help us feel better. It could be as simple as clearing clutter and rearranging furniture. Creating a space where we can relax and reflect can also be helpful. I have found that having plants and flowers around really helps to raise my mood.

FINDING GREATER MEANING IN LIFE

Taking time to get to know ourselves better can also help us develop greater meaning in our lives. Our great loss has given us the opportunity to change our lives for the better. Engaging in self-assessment will bring us closer to our inner guidance.

EXERCISE

SELF-ASSESSMENT FOR GREATER MEANING IN LIFE

Here are some things to ask yourself that can lead you to greater meaning in your life:

- What are the things that you love to do and that come easy to you? What qualities do you enjoy expressing the most in the world?
- What do you want to do? What are some of your hopes and desires?
- What do you want to say to loved ones or do with or for them?

When we journal about our fondest dreams and envision a more fulfilling way to be, we will find the voice of our Higher Self becoming more apparent.

WISDOM WE CAN GAIN FROM LOSS

As I reflect on my great loss, I am aware of several things that we can learn from such an experience. Most of us probably found that we coped with the tragedy better than we expected. The experience can awaken us to our inner strength, a resource that will fortify us for the future. We are awakened in other ways as well.

Experiencing the pain of our loss opens us up to the suffering of others. We become more sensitive and able to extend greater compassion to those who are hurting. For many of us, a simple recognition and acknowledgment of our pain has a healing, soothing effect. We no longer feel so isolated and invisible.

New pathways appear after a significant loss, and we tend to make major life adjustments. This may involve a career change, a move, or closer relationships. We often learn what is truly important to us after a significant loss. Great loss provides us with an opportunity to reevaluate the choices we have made and to put our time and energy into what is most important to us. Again, it is the whisperings of our Higher Self shining a light to show us the way during this dark time.

With the guidance of our Higher Self, we often choose to focus on something that gives us a sense of purpose and meaning after a significant loss. We are reminded of the satisfaction that can be had while helping others as we attempt to adjust to our loss. Helping others allows us to be fully present in the moment and may well be part of a higher purpose that we have set for ourselves. However, as in my case, a propensity to help others too much may have to be balanced, as you will see in the next chapter.

An excellent way to uncover the lessons from our loss is to make a connection with our Higher Self through a Life between Lives session, guided by a trained and certified Michael Newton Institute facilitator. Here are two examples from my practice.

HOW LOSS CREATES FREEDOM

Julie, an exercise physiologist and personal trainer in her mid-forties, had experienced a difficult year. First, her mother died after an extended period of poor health. Julie's relationship with her mother was a complicated one. Being the only daughter in the family, Julie was expected to be the main caretaker for her parents. Her two older brothers offered little in the way of support.

Her father, whom she was quite close to, had developed dementia and was now living in a nursing home. Thus, he was no longer able to offer her much support either. While she loved her mother, the situation had become quite burdensome. Her mother was a bit self-centered and very demanding.

However, Julie felt a strong sense of responsibility for the well-being of her parents and remained very attentive. While her mother had been in ill health for a while, her death at this time was not expected and was sad and disruptive for Julie.

The second thing that happened later the same year while Julie was still grieving the loss of her mother is that her five-year relationship with her boyfriend ended rather abruptly. While the relationship had not been all that she had wanted it to be, she harbored the hope that things would get better and that they could have a more committed relationship in the future. He told her that he had wanted to leave earlier, but then her mother died, so he had waited.

The way that he did tell her was hurtful and unanticipated. He simply announced that he was not in love with her and felt that it was time for him to move on. Shortly thereafter, he was in another relationship. Julie was shell-shocked.

Julie related that now the two main anchors in her life were gone and she suddenly felt adrift and alone. She hoped that a Life between Lives session could provide her with some insights and give her some direction for the future. She wanted to understand more about the meaning of the two relationships in her life that had taken up most of her time and energy no longer being there. To help her understand her current situation better, the guides took her to two past lives that were related to her current life.

J: *I am a black man with a spear in my hand and braided grass decorating my arms and neck and back. I'm in my forties and of average size. My name is Uganda.*

Dr. C: *Is anyone with you?*

J: *No, I am alone, and I am out hunting. I live on the plains. I must feed a lot of people, so I need to get it done. I am tired, but I must keep going. I am tired of having responsibility for so many people who are lazy and do not help.*

Dr. C: *Tell me about who you are responsible for feeding. Who does not help you?*

J: *My wife and my two children and others in the village. I am the boss, but no one else wants to do it, so I must do it. I want to run away and live by myself, but I cannot because I have responsibilities.*

Dr. C: *Uganda, I want you to look into the eyes of your wife and children and tell me if they are anyone from Julie's life.*

J: *My wife is Julie's mother, and my children are her brothers. I do not recognize the others.*

Dr. C: *Tell me what happens next.*

J: *I find large animals and kill one. Then I call out for someone to come from the village and help me carry the meat back. Several of the older boys finally come straggling and do help me.*

I feel good when I get back to the village because I brought them what they need. I want to leave, but I stay there and put up with the situation.

As time went by, Uganda got older and it became harder for him to keep going. Some of the older boys from the village started helping him more and wanted to learn to hunt. This gave him hope. His wife and children did not make it, and he gave more responsibility to the older boys he had been teaching to hunt. He would get very tired and did not feel well as he aged further. He died peacefully with the villagers around him in his sixties.

During the session, we were in contact with the Soul who was now Julie, and we asked that the Soul who had been Uganda and was now

Julie speak to us from the perspective of Uganda. We asked this to allow us to better understand the connection between the two lives in terms of the lessons being learned. We also asked for advice for Julie that would allow her to learn the lessons chosen for this lifetime.

U: *Things could be worse. You (Julie) are not trapped like I was. Stop thinking you are trapped. It is worth it to leave a life you are not happy in.*

Dr. C: *What did you learn from your life, Uganda? If you had your life to live over, would you do anything differently?*

U: *I would have left and found another village and another wife who was not lazy. Instead, I was a loner and I kept doing what was expected of me, but I resented all the responsibility put on me.*

  Julie can be free to be herself, like I was not. When people do not or cannot take responsibility for their lives, do not take it upon yourself anymore!

Dr. C (addressing the Soul and guides): *What guidance do you have for Julie?*

Higher Self: *Julie should get out and find new connections. She needs to quit being responsible for others. Do not repeat the past. Do not take on responsibility for others. It is a false honor, a trap keeping you stuck.*

  The guides then directed Julie to another past life to gain additional understanding regarding her current lessons.

J: *It is sunset and I am outside playing in front of the house, dressed up like Little Bo Peep. I am a six-year-old girl and I am play-acting. There is a white dog and I pretend he is a sheep. It's in the 1800s in England and my parents are very wealthy. My name is Jasmine, and my parents love me so much.*

Dr. C: *Tell me about your family, Jasmine.*

J: *My father is older and he is a banker. My mother is younger and sweet. I have a new baby brother. We are happy.*

Dr. C: *Do you recognize anyone in your family as someone from Julie's life?*

J: *Yes, my mom is Julie's mother, but she is sweet now. My baby brother is Julie's older brother now.*

Jasmine goes on to relate that she was close to her father as she grew up, and he encouraged her to make something of herself. He wanted her to go to college, and she was excited about that. She went to Paris to study art and visit museums. She hoped to teach art someday. She reports that she had a good experience at college.

Upon graduation, Jasmine decided to move to Paris and study art further at museums. She became an expert and took a job at a museum. There she worked with a man named Samuel from England who was interested in her. They became friends and eventually she agreed to marry him and return to England to live, although she was not excited about it. It was more that she thought that was what she should do to please her family. She says that she figured he would do, and she did need to marry someone.

Dr. C: *Look into Samuel's eyes and tell me if he is anyone from Julie's life.*

J (surprised): *Why, yes, he is my previous boyfriend, the one I moved to this area for. We broke up and he quickly married someone else.*

Dr. C: *Tell me how things go when you move back to England with Samuel.*

J: *We have three children who are happy and lively. My husband works for a university and I do some art consulting. We are reasonably content. It is the way it must be. Everything is normal.*

Dr. C: *Tell me how your parents and your brother are doing now.*

J: *My father dies, and my mother is getting older. My brother is a misfit and stays at home tending to mother. I am doing what is expected of me. It is not uncomfortable. I do not know how things could be any different. I am living a conventional life rather than a rebellious one. There is nothing to run from. I have such a good family. I went for certainty. Samuel is happy, but I am marking time. I do think a lot about what could have been though.*

I have these ideas about going into the city to a burlesque club. Samuel does not know. I do not go. I just have fantasies about rebelling. I would like to shock people, but I do not act on it. I feel that life is drab, but I do not do anything about it.

Jasmine went on to report that she died of a sudden illness while her children were still at home and her mother was still alive. Her family was very attentive during her brief illness. She says she knew that Samuel would take care of everyone after she was gone.

Again, we speak to the Soul who was Uganda, Jasmine, and now Julie, and ask to be given information from the perspective of Jasmine.

Dr. C: *Jasmine, what did you want to show or tell Julie about your life? What did you learn in that life?*

J: *I was born into a good family, with wealth, love, and kindness, and I still did not have the life I wanted. I would have been more likely to go out on my own if my family had not been so good. I would have asked for my father's support to go after my dreams. I wanted to be a curator of a museum eventually and have a unique and caring husband. I did not feel that I could have both.*

I want Julie to fulfill the dream that I did not get to follow. I do not want her to settle for doing what others think she should do. Go have adventures! Just because people like you does not mean you have to be with them.

Dr. C: *What guidance is available for Julie?*

Higher Self: *There is nothing to hold Julie back from having adventures. Her family was an anchor that kept her from pursuing her own dreams. There is nothing holding Julie back now; she is free.*

She has lost her responsibility for her mother and she has lost the boyfriend who was wrong for her. That relationship did not allow her the freedom to do what she wanted. It was not an anchor, but an anvil, keeping her trapped. Her relationship with her mother was oppressive. She has now been freed to do whatever she wants.

There will be others who will want to weigh you down. Feel the heart of others. Do not be fooled by your giving to others as constituting a relationship. The giving should be reciprocal.

Guides: *Losses have set Julie free, but it is scary being free. We suggest getting some encouragement from your father, because he believes in you, even if he has some memory loss. The other thing to do is to grieve. You need to mourn your losses and then take advantage of the freedom.*

We want her to know that she is being watched over even though there is no one currently on earth to love and encourage her. That is coming from many of us at home. All that weighs her down is gone now. She has the love and encouragement to go forward.

We learn from Julie's session that the painful loss we experienced may have been the thing that was holding us back from following the plans we had developed for ourselves for this lifetime. Once we have experienced the loss, we are free to pursue our own dreams. However, we must mourn our losses before we set off on our own life path.

We also learn that when we feel all alone because there is no one special to love and encourage us after our loss, we are not alone. There are many Souls back in our home in the spirit world who are sending us love and encouragement. We can make space to feel this love and encouragement to boost our confidence as we move forward on our life path. But we must remember that the most important thing we can do is to connect with our Higher Self for guidance and support and to love ourselves.

A REMINDER TO RETURN TO PURPOSEFUL LIVING

Daniel is a forty-three-year-old single parent who lost his wife, Joanna, the love of his life, years ago. He raised their son, who is now grown and has left home. Their daughter is still at home with him. He is very spiritual and has been able to connect with his wife in the afterlife. Before she died, they had agreed that when one of them died, they would let the other one know what the afterlife was like. They selected a password so they would know if they were in contact with each other. A family member who is a medium was able to give him the password when she attempted to help them connect. He came for a session to learn more about what to do with his life now. In response to our questions, the guides took him back to a past life that he shared with Joanna.

D: *I am a twelve-year-old boy standing on a dock in a river that goes to the ocean. My name is Nathan. I am barefoot and wearing short pants. I am looking out over the town, which has a lot of wooden buildings. It is a large port town in England, or maybe Scotland, by the name of Leven something. There are a few others here working on the docks. We are in front of a tall building that has a large front opening, and we are loading cargo to go on a ship.*

Dr. C: *Do you live close by?*

D: *We live close by in a room over a shop in town. There is my mom and dad and I have two older brothers and one younger brother, plus a sister. We do not see much of our father.*

Dr. C: *Nathan, do you recognize anyone in your family as someone in Daniel's life?*

D: *My sister is my little sister, and my mom is my current mom. My oldest brother is my grandfather now. Our family gets along well. We are poor, but we get by. I will not have shoes until my big brother grows out of them.*

Dr. C: *What is the next significant thing that happens in your life, Nathan?*

D: *My oldest brother gets sick from a disease that is going around and he dies. No one else in the family gets sick, but I leave and move to the country. When I was seventeen, I met Abiatha at church, and we got married. I am going to live with her family. Abiatha is Joanna!*

Things are much better now. We all live in separate houses on the family's land and we all work to support the family. Abiatha and I live a long and happy life and I die first. I did not want to go, but Abiatha told me it was okay.

My guide is telling me that we do not have any losses. We see each other again when we go back home to the spirit world. We visit with each other at night. We live other lives together. When we are here on earth, we just think that they are gone. The connection is always there.

My guide tells me that I have a strong connection with Joanna. I do hear her; I just need to trust myself. Joanna is a soul mate, and we have lived many lives together. We agreed that she would die early this time while we were here so that I could be more open to others.

Dr. C: *What else did Daniel hope to do during this lifetime?*

Guide: *He wanted to learn to let go of control. He can see that and is doing it well. He has had many circumstances in his life that he could not control. Each time that he just allowed things to happen, it got easier.*

Higher Self: *Daniel's life has a lot to do with love. Everything is about love. We come to earth to grow, to share love, and to have connections. We all get to learn. Sometimes parents are just there to get you to life on earth, but often there is a connection, like Daniel has with his daughter.*

We are always together in spirit. We are all energy. We just do not always come to earth together at the same time. Daniel is learning more about love. It is always there; we just need to be open to it. What seems to be bad is not bad. Just be open to love.

Our lives on earth are quick. When Daniel met Joanna here, he knew she was for him. He did not really learn anything from his older brother who died in his life as Nathan, but when he saw him again after his death, he learned that we are always connected. We always figure things out when we are in between lives.

Daniel became aware that Joanna was with us in the session, and he smiled broadly. He asked about a move for him and his daughter.

Joanna (laughing): *Quit being a wuss! You have got to quit being in control. Quit trying to organize everything. Just go and do it. Everything will work* *out. Do not worry about her. Anything that happens will happen away from here. Life is better than you expected.*

Daniel: *I want to find real joy.*

Joanna: *Let go of control. You have got a lot of years to live yet. Plenty of time. So shut up and listen to stay in contact with your Higher Self and guidance.*

Daniel: *Thank you, Joanna. You suffered a lot to teach me a lot. Your dying early was a brave choice.*

Joanna: *Leave it all behind. You are still holding on to too much. Walk away from everything that is today into tomorrow.*

Dr. C: *Daniel would like to have a signal to let him know when he is trying to control things.*

Daniel: *Joanna is laughing at me. She says a kick in the head.* (Daniel laughs too, delighted to be interacting with Joanna.)
I am being told that the guides will give me reminders. I just need to trust and quit thinking it is my imagination.
Our daughter is going to be fine, not easy, but we will always be close.

Dr. C: *Daniel would like to know if a new relationship is in his future.*

Daniel: *Joanna is encouraging me. It is there if I want it. It is no one I know now, but it will be like when I met Joanna.*

Dr. C: *Are there any additional messages for Daniel?*

Daniel: *The guides are telling me that it is time to get moving. Untie from the house and the job, and just let things go. Be ready when spirit calls. Be open to guidance. I need to let go of fear and listen. They are telling me I need to quit making distracting noise. I need to set an intention and listen!*
I see the image of a bull and a toreador with a red flag. I need to quit dodging and let the bull run me over.

Our departed loved ones may connect with us during a Life between Lives session. This is usually very emotional and has a lasting impact.

Daniel was tremendously uplifted and inspired by the encounter with Joanna. He related that he now felt ready to move forward and tackle the lessons of becoming more open to others and letting go of control. We also witnessed Joanna encouraging Daniel to have another romantic relationship. In Life between Lives sessions, I have often heard from the departed that they want their surviving spouse or partner to find love again and be happy.

I heard from Daniel shortly after the session. He had done some research and found the port town of Levenmouth, Scotland, right on a river that flows into the sea. Back in the 1800s, the docks were used for loading and shipping coal. He also reported that he had gone on a cruise with his sister and had met a woman for whom he felt an immediate attraction.

Often it is possible to connect with a lost loved one during a Life between Lives session. You can find a list of certified Michael Newton Institute Life between Lives facilitators at www.newtoninstitute.org. I share the important life lesson I discovered through a Life between Lives session in the next chapter.

Here are some strategies to learn the lessons contained in your great loss:

- Assess the quality of your life before your loss.
- Explore your forgotten hopes and dreams.
- Seek greater meaning in your life.
- Discover the wisdom that great loss can bring.
- Explore your life purpose and lessons through a Life between Lives session.

EXERCISE

EXPLORE YOUR FORGOTTEN HOPES AND DREAMS

Think back to earlier times in your life and remember what excited you, what you wanted to do but never got around to. Think about the things that you wanted to make sure you did before you die. Recall those activities that you enjoyed so much that you would lose track of time. What are the things you dream about doing someday? Write about them in your journal. When will the time for them be right? Maybe the time is now.

CHAPTER ELEVEN

LEARNING THE LESSONS OF LOSS

I am the only certified Life between Lives facilitator in my area and was fortunate to be able to schedule an in-person session at a gathering of practitioners at a Michael Newton Institute world conference during the summer following the unexpected death of my daughter. Had this conference not been scheduled, I could have done a remote session online. While it had not been quite a year and I was still grieving, I decided to make the trip anyway. There were parts of the gathering that I did not participate in, but the excursion proved to be beneficial. It was comforting to connect with my colleagues, but the most healing part was the Life between Lives session that I received.

The world conference brought certified members of the Michael Newton Institute together from all over the world. Thus, I was able to schedule a session with one of the most experienced and skillful members in the organization. Here I share with you the details of my session and the profound life lesson I was able to reap from the experience.

MY LIFE BETWEEN LIVES SESSION

I see a gorgeous young woman in a beautiful yellow and pink silk and satin gown. She has long, red hair. She is holding something that looks like a mirror, and she is fussing with her hair.

I am a baby, and I am in this boxlike thing. I am partially sitting up so that I can watch her. She is my mother. I do not see her much. My nanny is there too. She is wearing a long, coarse cloth dress and she has a head covering. My mother is my daughter in my current life and my nanny is my maternal grandmother.

I am a little older now and I am wearing a dress. I am still with my nanny. She drinks out of this brown jug and then falls asleep and slumps in the corner and snores. I am about four or five years old now. We live in this large stone building with stone floors. I can smell the smoke from the fireplaces that are in every room. We are in the Cornwall area of England and the year is 1882. My name is Catherine.

I explore while my nanny sleeps. I like to go to the room where my mother keeps her gowns and shoes. My mother is not around much. I feel abandoned. I do not understand why she does not want to be with me.

Now I am a teenager and I can have friends come to visit me. My nanny is still around, but I am more independent now. We go on picnics.

I do not see much of my mother. She has nothing to say to me. Father runs the land and he is always busy. He supervises the workers. He does not pay any attention to me either. I want to get away from here. I can have anything I want, but I do not get any attention.

I am fifteen years old now and my parents are talking about me marrying. They will choose a suitable husband for me. I feel invisible and I have no control over this. I do want to get out of here though, so I go along with it.

It is my wedding day and I have a beautiful gown and wonderful soft shoes. The husband they chose for me is older. His first wife died, and he has grown children. He seems nice enough, just boring. He has told me that I will have duties, managing the household and caring for the workers when they are sick. That will be okay, as I did not have anything to do before. My new husband is my current romantic partner.

I supervise the castle staff and take food and medicine to the workers when they are sick or when a baby is born. My husband is gone a lot. He is aloof and boring. It seems again that I can have whatever I want, but I do not get much attention.

I wanted to have children, but I do not. My husband really did not want to have any more children. I carry out my duties well.

My husband dies. His cousin comes to take over the land and I continue living there. The cousin is kind to me. I become older and I cannot do much anymore.

I am out for a walk around the castle one evening. I am not sick; I am just out enjoying the twilight. Then I start to feel different, sort of light-headed. It is as if my energy just leaves me, so I sit down. The next thing I know, I am looking down and I see myself below, motionless.

Now I see my Soul family welcoming me. There are also about a hundred others welcoming me home. I see among them some of the workers that I helped. They are all so welcoming. I feel warm.

They tell me all the ways that I helped them, how I brought them food. When my husband would beat the staff, I would go out to help them with herbal salves and tea. They are thanking me.

I learned in that life that maybe no one would pay any attention to me, but I could pay attention to them. After I figured this out, I never felt lonely again. I saw the suffering around me and knew that I could help. That was my fulfillment.

My Higher Self explains that helping others has been a major theme for me over several lifetimes. The challenge for me in this life is not to help so much that I do not take care of myself. Another part of this challenge is not to help others so much that they do not help themselves.

I helped my daughter too much. I made her feel like she couldn't do anything for herself.

Then I felt my daughter's energy, and it was if she had come to give me a hug. I felt enveloped in a profound warmth. It brought tears of joy to my eyes, and it was if a cold block of ice gave way inside my chest.

My daughter told me that in her eyes I had always looked perfect and I could do everything well. She went on to tell me that she was grateful for all the love and help I had given her, but she had felt helpless and out of control. She had come to feel very dependent on me.

My Higher Self gives me a deeper explanation. I am told that when I planned this lifetime, I needed a situation in which I could love someone unconditionally and allow them to follow their own path. This meant allowing them to make their own mistakes and experience the consequences so that they could learn and grow.

My daughter needed a situation in which she could experience love but be free to follow her own path. She had felt that she had no control in previous lives. So we agreed to come to earth together to help each other learn and grow.

My daughter and I had not had any contact in subsequent lives on earth since that time in England. When she showed up again with me on earth, I chose to connect in the helping way I had learned in that lifetime.

By the time I figured out that I was helping her too much, she had gone too far to get her life back. She had become so bogged down in destructive behavior and habits that she no longer had the will to try to turn her life around. So she left and went back home. I learned the lesson that we had planned together, but she will learn her part of that lesson in a future life.

My daughter and I had many lives on earth together before our time in England. She has had many dependent lives and realizes that she needs to become more independent, but she has not acted on it yet. She stayed long enough in this lifetime to learn what she needs to do. She will have a successful life in the future, and I will play a role in that life as well.

My daughter thanks me for giving her unconditional love. She is even thanking me for all the limits I set during the last years of her life. She tells me that it was not my fault. She has been struggling with addiction for several lifetimes. She knew that I would find out soon that she was taking a lot more than her prescription drugs, and she did not want to disappoint me.

My Higher Self tells me that I have spent lifetimes helping others too much. I start to see my imprudent helping behavior and set limits with the person I'm trying to help and then a tragedy occurs. This pulls me back into helping mode, but this time I learned the lesson. Helping others is a good thing, but it must be balanced with taking care of myself and allowing them to take care of themselves.

I was so grateful for the contact I was able to make with my daughter during this session and was overwhelmed by all the information given. I would like to be able to say that I took all the wisdom of the session to heart then, but that is not the case. I was still deeply grieving and unable to process it at that time.

I find that this is the case with many of my patients. It is only later that they discover the profound clear-sightedness of the information revealed to them during their Life between Lives sessions. Often I will hear from patients that they have just now realized, months or even years later, how life-changing the information revealed in their sessions was. Such was the case for me.

CLARITY REGARDING MY LESSON

It was over a year after my Life between Lives session that I started thinking about what had been revealed in the session and decided to listen to the recording. I was struck by the simple and profound nature of the information I had received. The words of one of my dissertation advisors came back to me. He said that knowledge that can be stated simply and directly is always the most profound. If it is too complicated, the message will be lost.

As I listened to the recording of my session, I realized how simple and clear the message was. I had helped my daughter too much, fostering her dependency. To do that, I'd had to let go of my own hopes and dreams. I had made the situation worse for both of us through my unrestrained helping behavior.

I learned from my session that I am drawn to help others because that is the way I learned to make connections in my past life in England, when I felt invisible and abandoned. Deep down I believed that helping those who were having problems was the best way for me to connect and feel a part of things, rather than feeling unnoticed and inconsequential. It was my conscious self that made this decision, and from that vantage point, I thought that I knew what was best for those I was helping. This pattern of behavior helped me feel good about myself and connected to those around me.

Over time I became stuck in this pattern of behavior, even though it was no longer appropriate or needed. Instead of stepping back and letting those whom I was helping take over when the time was right, I would just keep helping and giving. Putting myself and my needs first felt very greedy and selfish to me, because it was unfamiliar behavior. Neglecting my own needs caused me to feel drained and exhausted much of the time.

I felt so sorry for my daughter when I learned what had happened to her. I knew that she was going through a difficult time in her life, so I jumped in to help her move beyond that situation. In retrospect, I can see that I also felt frightened, as she seemed so vulnerable and broken after her traumatic experience. My fear was that I would lose her if I didn't do something to change the situation. At the time, my actions felt justified and even honorable to me. But I have learned that it does not really work that way.

Watching a loved one go through difficult times can be very painful. We instinctively want to help them and share what we have learned about hard times. Yet as Souls here having a human experience, we all have the right to follow our own path and learn our own lessons without any outside interference. Denying others this experience hampers their progress toward Soul enlightenment. We learn through experience. Although advice can be helpful, true insight that changes behavior at a core level is not conveyed in this manner.

I was so focused on helping my daughter get over this tragic incident that I ignored the strong evidence that she was becoming more dependent rather than making progress in her life. While she was telling me in many ways that she had given up, I refused to acknowledge it. What that might mean was just too painful for me to tolerate at the time. So I retreated into denial. I just kept thinking that if I tried harder and gave more, things would turn around. It took running into dead ends every way I tried to go that finally caused me to see where I was going wrong.

We all must learn by exercising our independence to make our own choices and then reflecting on the consequences of those choices. We honor others by allowing them to do this. Though we may not agree with their decisions, each of us must learn in our own way and according to our own timetable.

I had a difficult time accepting this. Rather than empathizing with my daughter's need to grow more autonomous, I kept trying to intervene for quite a while. Because of my denial, I did not realize until after her unexpected death that she was trying to tell me that she had given up and just did not want to try anymore. I did finally understand that I needed to allow her to face the consequences of her choices during this time, but I fully expected that she would use those experiences in a positive, constructive manner.

While I did learn to set limits and encourage healthy behavior in my daughter when she was still here on earth, I did not learn to care for myself properly then. There was a lot of joy in learning to do this after my time with her. I now consider what I need first before jumping in to meet the needs of others. Putting ourselves and our needs first does not mean that we are uncaring or self-absorbed. In fact, helping others can be more beneficial and authentic when we take care of ourselves first.

Healthy helping promotes other people's growth and independence and the development of their potential. Unhealthy or dysfunctional helping does just the opposite. In the end, misguided helping is a waste of our talents and resources and the precious time that we have on earth. When we see to our own needs first, we can then help others in a manner that is beneficial to both them and us.

Initially I was disheartened that while I did finally see the error of my ways and correct what I was doing, things still did not turn out the way I had hoped. Later, I became aware that those feelings were coming from my conscious self. My Higher Self, able to see the situation from a higher perspective, was delighted that I had finally learned that lesson.

Through tuning in to my inner guidance and establishing communication with the Soul who had been my daughter, I came to know that all was well. She had returned home to the loving embrace of her Soul family and the encouragement and assistance of her guides and wise spiritual helpers. She was now recovering from what had been a difficult earth incarnation and was preparing to return in the future to complete the learning that she had started.

Through making repeated mistakes, I finally learned the lesson embedded in the unfolding events in my life. Life on earth can seem to be difficult. However, if we acknowledge that the hardships we encounter on our path are there to help us learn and grow, we can view them in a more positive light. Perceiving an obstacle that we encounter as a tool for growth makes our journey as a Soul easier.

It is also helpful to remember that hardships are things that we have chosen so that we can learn to overcome them, not things that happen to us to make us miserable. Life on earth is a captivating adventure for the brave Soul.

As I continued to tune in to my inner guidance, I began to understand more about how off-base I had been in my attempts to help my daughter. I did get the unconditional loving part right, and my intention to help was on target. I just did not know how to help her get to a place that would allow her to understand her situation and create her own solutions. That scenario would have empowered her and enabled her to deal with similar situations in the future. Following our inner guidance can help us approach situations such as these from the Soul's perspective.

THE SOUL'S PERSPECTIVE
ON HELPING OTHERS

It is only our conscious self, or ego, that wants to impose our solutions to problems on others. The Soul does not impose anything on others, yet it does help them.

The Soul looks at the person and feels deeply for them. The Soul is then able to see the situation from the perspective of the other Soul and acknowledge and support them in facing the challenge before them. This helps the person free themselves from fear, and once free from fear, they can make choices that are right for them.

This is what helping is all about from the Soul's perspective. It is not about giving opinions, making decisions, or solving other people's problems for them. It is not about giving them things they should be securing for themselves or protecting them from the consequences of their actions.

Real help, from this perspective, is about enabling the other Soul to shine. We can do this by extending love and compassion to them. We can also give them encouragement and let them know they are not alone in their struggles. The goal is to make them feel good about themselves and awaken them to their personal power. From the Soul's perspective, there is never any judgment involved when helping others.

When we help others by empowering them and enriching their lives, we are raising the consciousness on earth. Easing the suffering of another in any way, no matter how small, is among the loftiest of goals and a gift to ourselves. By raising the vibration of others, we raise the vibration within ourselves. We cannot help all who need it, but we can leave the earth a better place than how we found it.

All of us make mistakes as we live our lives here on earth. The Soul and our spiritual helpers never judge or shame another for making mistakes.

We are expected to make mistakes. It is the wise Soul who always learns from them.

Placing yourself in another's shoes and imagining the advice or help that you would like to receive if you were that person is a way that we can show empathy. When we treat others as we would like to be treated, we are less likely to make a mistake in our helping behavior.

We must remember that in earth school, we are not always going to give the right answers or act in the most appropriate manner. We might hurt others. It is important that we forgive ourselves for our errors. When I realized how I had fostered my daughter's dependence rather than empowering her, I felt ashamed and unworthy. From the Soul's perspective, however, there is never any blame.

For me, healing from these negative emotions meant apologizing to the Soul who was my daughter and forgiving myself. I also realized that I had to forgive her for the struggles that she put me through during the last years of her life on earth and the heartache that I experienced. Forgiving her was easy, but forgiving myself was difficult.

It was hard for me to forgive myself, as I tended to excuse her behavior and feel responsible for the things that happened. But that attitude did not lead to healing. As I continued to work on forgiving myself, I discovered that I felt guilty for not realizing that she had been using illegal drugs and getting her help before it was too late.

UNPRODUCTIVE GUILT AND
THE POWER OF FORGIVENESS

Guilt does have a purpose, because it helps us understand when we have done something to harm someone. However, after we identify the reason that we feel guilty, apologize for it if necessary, and reflect on the situation to prevent a similar one in the future, continuing to feel guilty becomes unproductive. Unproductive guilt serves no purpose and just makes us feel bad.

Instead, we can change our guilt into gratitude. We can be thankful for the learning that we acquired from the situation. Once I established communication with my deceased daughter, I was able to tell her about how guilty I was feeling and ask for her forgiveness. Her loving response helped me let go of the guilt and appreciate what I had learned from the situation. You can ask for forgiveness indirectly at the Soul level without having a conversation and still achieve relief from your guilt. The important thing is to learn from your experience.

Forgiveness for ourselves as well as for others is vitally important in our healing journey. From the perspective of the Soul, we do not want to carry guilt or resentment back to the spiritual realm when we return home. I have learned through Life between Lives sessions that failure to clear negative energy such as this is a source of regret for many Souls and may lead to unwanted karmic entanglements. It is important that we clear these feelings while we are still here on earth.

Despite my difficulties with helping behavior, I still believe strongly in helping others. What I have learned is that help must be given in a manner that does not prevent me from caring for myself properly or discourage others from helping themselves. I have also learned that when we help others, there should be no expectations attached to the act. While I already knew these things intellectually, it was my great loss that enabled me to internalize and live this Soul wisdom.

When we help others, we are also helping ourselves. When we give unconditionally, we keep the energy flowing and raise the vibration on earth. When we give selflessly, we increase abundance and gratitude in all the lives that we touch. We are here to help each other, and this behavior nourishes us as Souls. Making others feel good about themselves is one of the greatest gifts we can give.

Dr. Michael Newton tells us that to be effective in our mission, we are expected to help others on their paths whenever possible. He warns against becoming too self-absorbed. Helping others in ways that empower them is one of our highest callings.

FINDING YOUR LIFE LESSONS

I describe my lesson regarding helping behavior as an example. Your lessons are unique to you. We have all chosen to come to earth to learn lessons that are difficult to learn back home in the spirit world. We may have been trying to learn these lessons over many lifetimes. Great loss provides us with a unique opportunity to stop on the path that we have been on, take stock of our lives, and connect with our inner guidance. Doing so will help us find and learn our lessons.

If we view our loss from a spiritual perspective, we remember that we are here to learn and grow. Before we incarnated, we planned what we wanted to learn in our upcoming life. The circumstances of our life—our family, relationships, opportunities, and challenges—were all chosen by us to enable us to learn these lessons.

An important part of our earth experience is the opportunity to make mistakes and learn from their consequences. We may be shamed by others for making mistakes here on earth. The beauty of the spiritual realm, as I have come to understand it from my practice and my own experiences, is that we are never judged, but rather are lovingly assisted to learn through experience.

I have pondered how we learn our life lessons at the core level so that they serve as a guide for our behavior in the future. While I have long understood healthy and unhealthy helping behavior intellectually, I still engaged in unhealthy helping behavior with my daughter. I learned that this was a problem I had been struggling with for many lifetimes. What I experienced in uncovering this lesson was that I was blind to how I was acting in a way that was contrary to what I knew intellectually to be true. My overdeveloped sense of responsibility as a parent was one of the things that got in the way of me seeing this.

While I am still exploring this topic, I have noticed that, as Souls, we plan increasingly challenging circumstances in our incarnations to help us learn these perplexing lessons. A key to success appears to be following our inner guidance as we navigate these challenges.

Out Higher Self lovingly and patiently waits for our conscious self to wake up and learn from the experiences we are having during our earth incarnation. We also have infinitely patient spiritual guides who love us and steer us toward what is in our best interest. We receive love and encouragement from our ancestors and our departed loved ones. While we are often subjected to judgment here on earth, there is no judgment in our real home.

However, as we are learning to tune in to our inner guidance in a more effective manner, there are some clues to look for in finding our life lessons. For example, we all have gifts or things that we do well and that come easy to us, but there can be a downside to them that we do not see. I am very good at helping people, but the downside for me is that I can help people past the point where they should be helping themselves, and I do so by sacrificing my own well-being. My lesson was to learn healthy helping behavior and maintenance of my own self-care. Look at your gifts and ponder whether there is a downside to them that you may be blinded to in your own behavior.

Another thing to look for is any emotionally charged situation or circumstance in your life. If you have a strong emotional reaction to something that happens or that someone says, step back and look at the situation more closely. There might be a life lesson behind your reaction that you do not yet see.

Be on the alert for repeating patterns in your life. Does the same situation keep happening at different times, with different people, or in different circumstances? If so, take some time to reflect on what might be occurring and what your role in it might be.

Here are some suggestions for finding your life lessons:

- Focus on problems, fears, and situations that are stressful to you, particularly those related to your loss. Things in our lives that we find challenging, frustrating, or irritating are keys to our life lessons. Also look for recurring difficulties and obstacles. Notice any knee-jerk reactions you have to anything someone points out to you. Choose one or more that seem most significant in your current life to examine more closely.

- Acknowledge that the issues you have identified are problematic, and spend time reflecting on them. You may wish to record your thoughts in your notebook. As we accept our problems and challenges and contemplate them, insights and solutions tend to arise.

- Ask for guidance from your Higher Self and spirit helpers. Accessing spiritual wisdom and support through contact with our Higher Self and our spiritual helpers is very healing. We can achieve this by ourselves or with the assistance of spiritual facilitators such as mediums or oracle cards, as described in previous chapters.

- Face possible denial on your part by accepting responsibility for the difficulty. This requires courage and the desire to know the truth. Try to identify underlying beliefs you may have about the issue and then challenge your assumptions. Introspection into the possible cause of the problem may also be helpful. Facing the truth may feel humiliating, painful, or frightening, but this is an opportunity to face your vulnerabilities and achieve peace.

- Schedule a Life between Lives session with a certified Michael Newton Institute facilitator. You will be allowed to ask questions during your session. Pose questions that enable you to gain an understanding of the issues, the nature of your lessons, attitudes that will be useful, and actions that will demonstrate the mastery of your lessons.

We are all on our own life path and have free will to direct our life on earth. We can choose to pass or fail a lesson in earth school. While we can shape the events in our own life, ultimately we have no control over the path others choose to take. This is not a cause for despair, because we never lose the connection with our loved ones. While I wish that my daughter could still be here with me on earth, I now have a much better understanding of the situation and why she went back home early.

Our time on earth is short. We are here to learn and grow, and this knowledge allows me to be grateful for the lesson I learned even in the face of my loss. I know that I am still connected to the precious Soul who was my daughter and I will see her again. The love we shared remains, and that sustains me. The Life between Lives session let me know that she, too, made progress in this lifetime through learning that it is time for her to be more independent. I have no doubt that she will accomplish that soon.

Great loss comes into our lives to free us from patterns that are limiting our growth. This gives us a second chance to accomplish the goals and learn the lessons that we set for this lifetime. What appears to be a setback is really a clearing of the road ahead of us.

Here are some things you can do to discover your life lessons following great loss:

- Identify problems or issues that have become apparent following your great loss.
- Contemplate or meditate on the issues.
- Ask for spiritual guidance in resolving the problems.
- Choose to confront the issues.
- Explore the possibility of denial or faulty assumptions on your part.
- Schedule a Life between Lives session.

EXERCISE

REFLECT ON ISSUES REVEALED BY YOUR LOSS

Challenges created by your loss may hold the key to the identification of lessons that you planned for this incarnation. Look carefully at the issues related to these challenges and consider what you can learn as you work to resolve them. Ask for spiritual guidance as you contemplate them. Write about this in your notebook.

- Make note of the emotions that arise as you focus on these issues or problems.

- Look at your gifts and accomplishments and consider whether there is a downside to them that contains a lesson for you.

- Reflect on emotionally charged situations that you encounter.

- Look for patterns in which the same issue or problem keeps appearing at different times or in different circumstances.

Is there a lesson embedded in any of these cases?

CHAPTER TWELVE
LIFE BEYOND GREAT LOSS

Freed by our great loss from the patterns that were limiting our spiritual growth, we now have the chance to live our best life yet. After loss, we have the option to reinvent our life and ourselves. Tomorrow is a new day with new opportunities. It is essential to start building new dreams, new memories, and basically a new life.

What I have discovered through my healing journey is that we are absolutely the most important person in our universe. Our relationship with ourselves is a critical factor in shaping the life that we live. We can turn our great loss into renewed motivation and growth and make our life better than ever.

We will never forget who or what we have lost. However, through actions to bring about healing and the passage of time, we can integrate this loss into who we are as a person. This experience will enrich our Soul character and be reflected in our human experiences in this lifetime and future lifetimes on earth.

GETTING IN TOUCH WITH WHO WE ARE

It is imperative that we get to know our real self, raise our self-esteem, and develop self-love. This requires a strong connection with our Higher Self, as this is who we really are on the inside. An invitation implicit in our great loss is for our conscious self and our Higher Self to join together to become our authentic self as we live out our days on earth. This will enable us to achieve the purpose that we set for this incarnation and learn the lessons that we planned. It will also enable us to create a life that is joyful and fulfilling as we complete the remainder of our days on earth.

Our reality depends on the extent to which we can forge this connection to our inner guidance and how much we love and take care of ourselves. Taking time to get in touch with who we are as an individual and connecting with our Higher Self is an important way to begin our journey into life after our loss.

Through listening regularly to our inner guidance, we can get back in touch with our hopes, dreams, and ambitions. Understanding what we want and where we want to go in life is crucial to being happy and reconnecting with the purpose that we set for this incarnation. Securing this connection to our inner guidance will take time, and maintaining it is a lifelong process. We can foster this process by caring lovingly for ourselves.

LOVING AND CARING FOR OURSELVES

Loving ourselves is more than a state of mind; it is a series of actions. It includes being kind and patient with our thoughts and ideas. We also need to forgive ourselves when we make mistakes. That is just a part of the growth process here on earth. Taking the space we need so that we have room to grow is essential.

Accepting our emotions without judging them is a loving way to listen to and care for ourselves. Our feelings are valid and should be honored. There is always a reason for the emotions that we experience. When we suppress our emotions, they are left to intensify inside of us.

Taking time to understand our feelings can help us get to know ourselves better and move forward in our lives.

A way to raise our self-esteem and regain our confidence is to do an inventory of our talents and strengths. These are the gifts that we can share with others. We should acknowledge our special abilities and nurture them. We tend to take them for granted, but they let us know how we can make our special contributions to the world. Doing so produces a wonderful sense of well-being.

It is also important to surround ourselves with positive and uplifting people. I have heard it said that we become more like the people we spend the most time with. Thus, we want them to be ones who will inspire us and encourage our personal growth.

For us as Souls to thrive, we need to be in an environment of love and harmony. We may need to set healthy boundaries with some people in our lives or even walk away from relationships that no longer fit us. Life is too short for us to be with others who make it difficult for us to create the life that we desire.

GETTING RID OF LIMITING IDEAS

Sometimes we hold on to ideas that can limit our growth. Changing old attitudes can open us up to new experiences. Here are a few new perspectives to counter notions that may be inhibiting our progress:

- The present is not an indicator of what the future will be like. After a loss, it is common to feel that life will always be sad and discouraging. That is simply not the case. When we choose to go after a better life, our future can be much brighter. Our great loss has freed us to move on to a better life.
- Feeling vulnerable is not a sign that we are headed in the wrong direction. This is a sign of fear rather than an indication of the "rightness" of our intended direction. Fear does not exist in our home in the spirit world. It is something that we learn here on earth. Fear is a challenge for us to overcome with assistance from our Higher Self. Vulnerability is often

encountered on the path to a renewed life. We must be willing to step out of our comfort zone and confront our fears.

- Being by ourselves is not something to be avoided. It is important for us to get comfortable spending time alone with ourselves. The only person we can really rely on is our own self. Happiness can only come from within. We must stop seeking someone or something outside of ourselves to be happy. Connecting with our Higher Self and our inner guidance will show us the way.

- Fitting in is not necessarily a good thing. We chose to incarnate here on earth for a specific purpose. We chose the correct circumstances in which to learn specific lessons. If we stray from our path because of peer pressure, wanting to fit in, a need for acceptance, or a fear of judgment or discrimination, then the choices made and the energy put into this life by our Higher Self will be for naught.

- Feeling all alone is just an illusion. We are never alone. It is appealing for Souls to come to earth to learn lessons in a lifetime where we perceive that we are alone. We can make great strides in our spiritual growth by doing so. It is also daunting, as our Soul's natural state is to be one with everything and the idea of being alone is frightening. These feelings of separateness are real while we are here living on earth so that we can learn, but the feeling of aloneness is just an illusion. We are still one with the whole; the only thing that is different is that we have agreed to participate in earth school and experience the illusion of separateness.

TAKING ADVANTAGE OF SPIRITUAL GUIDANCE

Two ways that we can connect with the spiritual guidance that is available to all of us are (a) to pay attention to our intuition and (b) to develop a relationship with our spirit guides. These are rich resources to guide us as we are reformulating our life after a great loss.

As spiritual beings having a human experience, we agree to forget about our divine heritage while we are living our life on earth. We carry this divinity within us as our Higher Self, and one of the ways that our real self speaks to us is through our intuition. When we listen to our intuition, we normally feel happy. If we ignore it, a wave of uneasiness may come over us. As one of my patients put it, "When I feel uneasy, I know my intuition is trying to tell me something."

It is important to pay attention to your intuition. There is a reason that a thought keeps popping up in your head. Your intuition is trying to speak to you. Be receptive to these subtle nuances. Note those times when the thought will not go away and you have a sense that you should do something. Life will flow much easier when you do this.

You will know that your intuition is speaking to you when you feel inspired and excited. Our intuition is always there to guide us in the right direction. So note those times when your mind keeps wandering back to the same thought. The more you listen to your intuition, the happier and more secure you will feel. There is a hypnotherapy recording on my website, www.healingfromgreatloss.com, designed to help you get in touch with your intuition.

When we add the ability to receive assistance from our spirit guides to our intuition, our lives work even better. Our guides never tell us what to do or make decisions for us, but they are always there for us. They love us, know us very well, watch over us, and always want what is best for us. They can nudge us to notice things, bring people and opportunities into our lives, and create serendipitous experiences for us. We all have one primary guide who is with us for our entire life. Other guides come to assist us for specific purposes. One such instance is to help us cope with loss.

Books have been written about meeting and working with our spirit guides, but I would like to offer some simple suggestions. Guides almost always offer information and answer questions during Life between Lives sessions. One of the questions that patients frequently ask is "What is the best way to communicate with my guides?" While there is some variation in the answers that spirit guides give to this question during sessions, their responses are remarkably consistent.

First, our spiritual guides want us to know that our primary guide is always with us and open to communicating with us. Most of us have more than one guide working with us, especially during difficult times in our lives, such as our great loss experience. Second, they want us to know that when we need guidance or assistance, all we need to do is ask. Our requests will not always be responded to in the manner that we expect, but we will be heard and given a response that is for our highest good. Our guides are always working in the background, helping us in unseen ways.

The simple advice I have heard repeatedly in sessions is that we should ask for help and guidance when we need it and then be open to receiving it. This requires us to be present and aware. I have also witnessed that the more we ask for guidance and pay attention to it, the more assistance we will receive. There are additional resources designed to help you connect with your spirit guides at www.healingfromgreatloss.com.

I suggest that you set an intention to communicate with your spirit guides and then meditate or listen in quiet reflection. It may also be helpful to write down your thoughts, because many times we can channel information from our guides in this manner. If you remain unsure whether you are making contact with your guides, ask for a sign.

You can call on your spirit guides anytime. Spirit guides are truthful, loving, and compassionate and are dedicated to helping us navigate the course we have chosen for ourselves during our time on earth. Make it a habit to ask your spirit guides for assistance. You may wish to make a list of the things with which you would like help. It is important to pay attention to the guidance you receive and to be grateful for the information received.

Trust the information that you receive. The decision as to what to do with the information is always left up to us. If you do decide to follow the guidance, release your expectations for a specific outcome and trust in a plan that is better than your own.

Next I share one of my patient's stories about how she found happiness again after her great loss.

RENEE'S STORY

In recalling her divorce some years ago, Renee told me that she thought that divorce was a worse experience than death. Fascinated by her comment, I asked her to tell me more. She stated that a death is sad, but when a divorce occurs, especially one that you did not see coming or did not want, you also feel betrayed and lied to. She said that she had felt worthless, unloved, and abandoned after the divorce and that she had cried every day for three years. At the time of our session, she looked so happy and satisfied with her life. I wanted to know more, so I asked her to share her story with me.

> *I had planned to go to college when I graduated from high school, but then I met Larry. He was tall, dark, and handsome, and I fell into lust as much as love. We were married less than a year later. He had finished college by then and became a high school math teacher and a coach. I settled happily into being a homemaker.*
>
> *The next year we had our first child, a daughter, and then a son two years later. I could not have been happier. Taking care of the children, cooking, cleaning, and managing the household became a source of great pride for me. I was good at it and was happy and content with my marriage and family. When the children were in high school and becoming more independent, I went to work in an office of a large corporation. Life was good.*
>
> *A couple of years later, I got a call at work from a woman I did not know. She asked me if I was happily married, and I responded that, yes, I was. Then she asked me if my husband had ever cheated, and I told her not that I knew. She went on to tell me that my husband was seeing her daughter and that she was trying to break it up. She told me that when he was telling me what he was doing, he was really seeing her daughter. She shared with me that her husband had strayed, but she*

forgave him and they were able to work it out. She wanted my help in breaking them up.

I was stunned when I hung up the phone, and I really did not believe her. My husband and I were still getting along so well, and nothing had really changed. I called to meet my husband for lunch and told him about the phone call. Of course, he denied everything, and I believed him.

After that, things did change. He became more distant. The next weekend he told me that he had to go to his office to finish some work that he had to have done by Monday. I followed him, and sure enough, he did not go to the office, but went to meet a sixteen-year-old girl. I was devastated but hoped that there still was an explanation.

I had planned to confront him the following weekend, but he moved out before I could do that. He told me that it was all a lie, but he was going to move in with his aunt for a while so he could find himself. He assured me that it had nothing to do with me; it was him. All our friends and family were shocked because they thought we were so in love. He just lied to them too.

After that, I learned that he had cheated on me before. The sixteen-year-old got pregnant and they arranged an abortion. Then he asked for a divorce because he planned to marry her. She had been one of his students. After that, he ignored not just me but the children as well.

I spent three years in therapy, until one day I decided that I just had to shape up. My boss offered me a transfer to one of our offices in another city. I jumped at the chance, knowing it was time for a new beginning. I left everything behind and made the move. I felt better almost right away, although I still cried a lot when I was by myself.

I started meditating, reading spiritual books, and going for long walks in nature. I did a lot of self-reflection. I started thinking, "This is just something I need to go through. It is beyond my control." So I decided to let my feelings out until they were all gone. During that time, I forgave my husband and made a promise to myself that I would be happy again.

I did go a bit crazy for a while, going out, drinking a lot, and having one-night stands. It was because of my feelings of abandonment. I had some relationships but did not marry again. My family ended up moving to the new city to be with me. I made a lot of friends, have become very spiritual, and have found contentment. My life is good again, maybe better than it has ever been. I know myself and my strengths now.

Renee's story illustrates how life after great loss can be very peaceful and incredibly good again. Her move mirrors what I have heard from many of my patients following loss. It seems that new surroundings, whether they be from an actual move or from redecorating and moving things around a bit, seem to raise the spirits. I did not actually move after my loss, but I rearranged the furniture and repurposed my daughter's room. She encouraged me to do that in our afterlife conversations.

Renee took the time to fully experience her feelings and spent a lot of time in self-reflection. As a result, she came to a place of acceptance and forgiveness as her spirituality deepened.

Renee's path to this feeling of contentment was not an easy one, but the growth she experienced through feeling her emotions fully, learning to forgive, and deepening her spirituality is inspiring. I wish you a successful ending to your great loss story as well. May you be richly blessed in your life after loss.

Here are some things you can do to make your life after loss even better than before:

- Get to know your real self and follow your inner guidance.
- Love and care for yourself.
- Let go of limiting ideas.
- Take advantage of spiritual assistance.

EXERCISE

EXPLORE ANY LIMITING IDEAS YOU MAY HOLD

Look honestly at your feelings about the future and what is possible for you. Write about this in your notebook.

- Do you feel that things will never get any better in your life?
- Do you think that when you fear something, you are being prevented from making a mistake?
- Do you feel that it is important to avoid being alone?
- Do you think that it is important to try to fit in, even if the situation or environment does not seem right for you?
- Do you feel all alone in the world?

CONCLUSION

Great loss comes into our lives to free us from patterns that are limiting our spiritual growth. It gives us the freedom to return to the purpose that we chose for this incarnation if we choose to grasp this opportunity. It also provides us with the time and space to learn the lessons that we planned for this lifetime.

While the shock and pain of the loss is something that we must overcome, the healing process can free us not only from the agony of this loss, but also from the hurt of previous losses in our life that have been weighing us down. A determined effort to come to terms with our loss restores our wings and, when successfully accomplished, allows us to fly into our destiny. As healing takes place, we don't really recover from our loss, but rather we integrate the experience of the loss into who we are. This enriches our Soul character and makes us a more empathetic and compassionate person.

The gift of great loss is a golden opportunity to align our conscious self with our Higher Self in order to become our authentic, or true, self.

This allows us to benefit from the inner guidance and spiritual assistance that is available to all of us as we live out our days on earth.

Yes, we can heal, and life can be better than it has ever been. But we still carry around a tiny sore spot deep inside from our great loss that never goes away. Most of the time we are not even aware that it is there, but then something touches us. It might be something we see that is beautiful or tender or something we hear someone say. It is something that moves us in a way that connects with that small spot of pain that we still carry buried deep inside. It brings tears to our eyes and a lump to our throat.

We get a flash of the intense pain we once felt, but only a glint. There is a momentary yearning for what was, but it fades away quickly. If we take the time to explore these feelings, another one is likely to emerge. That is a feeling of gratitude for the love and/or passion that we once experienced. That we get to keep. It is never really gone but remains a part of us, and we are forever richer for it.

As time passes, so does my gratitude for the time I did have here on earth with the wonderful Soul who was my daughter. What a fabulous adventure we had! I look forward to the day when I will see her again. But I'm not ready to return home just yet. The adventure continues.

BIBLIOGRAPHY

Cannon, Dolores. *Between Life and Death*. Huntsville, AR: Ozark Mountain Publishers, 1993.

Hogan, R. Craig, et al. *Afterlife Communication*. Loxahatchee, FL: Academy for Spiritual and Consciousness Studies Publications, 2014.

James, John W., and Russell Friedman. *The Grief Recovery Handbook*. 20th anniversary expanded ed. New York: William Morrow, 2009.

Moody, Raymond, Jr., with Paul Perry. *Glimpses of Eternity*. New York: Guideposts, 2010.

Michael Newton Institute, Ann J. Clark, Karen Joy, Marilyn Hargreaves, and Joanne Selinske. *Llewellyn's Little Book of Life Between Lives*. Woodbury, MN: Llewellyn, 2018.

———. *Wisdom of Souls*. Woodbury, MN: Llewellyn, 2019.

Newton, Michael. *Destiny of Souls*. St. Paul, MN: Llewellyn, 2000.

———. *Life Between Lives: Hypnotherapy for Spiritual Regression*. St. Paul, MN: Llewellyn, 2004.

———. *Journey of Souls*. St. Paul, MN: Llewellyn, 1994.

Newton, Michael, ed. *Memories of the Afterlife.* Woodbury, MN: Llewellyn, 2009.

Peters, William. "What Are Shared Crossings?" Shared Crossing Project. Accessed August 7, 2021. https://www.sharedcrossing.com/shared -crossings.html.

Pitstick, Mark. SoulPhone Foundation. "SoulPhone Device Overview," https://www.thesoulphonefoundation.org/soulphone-overview/, and "SoulPhone Project Updates," https://www.thesoulphone foundation.org/soulphone-update/. Accessed August 7, 2021.

Weiss, Brian L, MD. *Many Lives, Many Masters.* New York: Simon & Schuster, 1988.

———. *Through Time into Healing.* New York: Simon & Schuster, 1992.

RECOMMENDED RESOURCES

Ann J. Clark, PhD, RN, author website with additional resources,
   https://www.healingfromgreatloss.com

Afterlife Research and Education Institute, https://www.afterlife
   institute.org

The Michael Newton Institute, https://www.newtoninstitute.org

The Grief Recovery Method, https://www.griefrecoverymethod.com

ESTABLISHING AFTERLIFE COMMUNICATION
WITH A LOST LOVED ONE

Dillard, Sherrie. *I'm Still with You: Communicate, Heal & Evolve with Your
   Loved One on the Other Side.* Woodbury, MN: Llewellyn, 2020.

Fein, Judith. *How to Communicate with the Dead: And How Cultures Do It
   Around the World.* Santa Fe, NM: GlobalAdventure.us, 2019.

Hogan, R. Craig. "Self-Guided Afterlife Connections." Afterlife
   Research and Education Institute, Inc. Program available at http://
   selfguided.spiritualunderstanding.org. Accessed August 7, 2021.

Hogan, R. Craig, et al. *Afterlife Communication*. Loxahatchee, FL: Academy for Spiritual and Consciousness Studies Publications, 2014.

Holland, John. *Bridging Two Realms: Learn to Communicate with Your Loved One on the Other Side*. Carlsbad, CA: Hay House, 2018.

Lambright, Claudia. *Just a Dream Away: After-Death Communication Through Dreams*. Self-published, 2020.

Lippincott, Chris. *Spirits Beside Us: Gain Healing and Comfort from Loved Ones in the Afterlife*. Glossarium, 2020.

Mathews, Patrick. *Only a Thought Away: Keeping in Touch with Your Loved Ones in Spirit*. Woodbury, MN: Llewellyn, 2019.

Perl Migdol, Sheri. "The EVP Slideshow." http://www.sheriperl.com/evpguide.

Pitstick, Mark. SoulPhone Foundation. "SoulPhone Device Overview," https://www.thesoulphonefoundation.org/soulphone-overview/, and "SoulPhone Project Updates," https://www.thesoulphone foundation.org/soulphone-update/.

Ragan, Lyn. *Signs from Pets in the Afterlife: Identifying Messages from Pets in Heaven*. Atlanta, GA: Lyn Ragan, 2015.

Robertson, Blair. *Afterlife: Three Easy Steps to Connecting and Communicating with Your Deceased Loved Ones*. Phoenix, AZ: Aberdeenshire, 2019.

MINDFULNESS

Nhat Hahn, Thich. *Happiness: Essential Mindfulness Practices*. Berkeley, CA: Parallax Press, 2005.

———. *You Are Here: Discovering the Magic of the Present Moment*. Boston, MA: Shambhala, 2010.

Smalley, Susan L., and Diana Winston. *Fully Present: The Science, Art, and Practice of Mindfulness.* Cambridge, MA: Da Capo Press, 2010.

Sockolov, Matthew. *Practicing Mindfulness: 75 Essential Meditations to Reduce Stress, Improve Mental Health, and Find Peace in the Everyday.* Emeryville, CA: Althea Press, 2018.

Steginus, Melissa. *Everyday Mindfulness: 108 Simple Practices to Empower Yourself and Transform Your Life.* TCK Publishing, 2020.

TO WRITE TO THE AUTHOR

If you wish to contact the author or would like more information about this book, please write to the author in care of Llewellyn Worldwide Ltd. and we will forward your request. Both the author and the publisher appreciate hearing from you and learning of your enjoyment of this book and how it has helped you. Llewellyn Worldwide Ltd. cannot guarantee that every letter written to the author can be answered, but all will be forwarded. Please write to:

Ann J. Clark
℅ Llewellyn Worldwide
2143 Wooddale Drive
Woodbury, MN 55125-2989
Please enclose a self-addressed stamped envelope for reply,
or $1.00 to cover costs. If outside the U.S.A., enclose
an international postal reply coupon.

Many of Llewellyn's authors have websites with additional
information and resources. For more information,
please visit our website at http://www.llewellyn.com.

NOTES

NOTES

NOTES

NOTES

NOTES